Benchmark ADVANCE

Texts *for* English Language Development

BENCHMARK EDUCATION COMPANY

Table of Contents

Topic 1:
Government for the People 2

Topic 2:
Ways Characters Shape Stories 22

Topic 3:
Animal Adaptations 42

Topic 4:
Comparing Points of View 62

Topic 5:
Advancements in Technology 82

Topic 6:
Making Decisions 102

Topic 7:
Communities Then and Now 122

Topic 8:
Weather and Climate 142

Topic 9:
Spending Time and Money 162

Topic 10:
Forces and Interactions 182

Common Core State Standards 202

California English Language
Development Standards 205

Essential Question

Why do people participate in government?

Citizens work to keep our roads and bridges safe.

My Language Objectives

- Understand the language of cause and effect
- Use concrete and abstract nouns
- Write an informative essay
- Form and use irregular verbs
- Understand subject/verb agreement

My Content Objectives

- Build vocabulary related to government
- Understand why people participate in government

President
Lyndon Johnson

Dr. Martin
Luther King Jr.

Many Americans have worked
hard to protect people's rights.

VOTE

Every citizen has a
responsibility to vote.

3

Working Together by Sarah Glasscock

The National Weather Service predicted that bad flooding would hit Fargo, North Dakota...

So elected officials from the federal, state, and city governments met....

They wanted to keep water out of homes and businesses, and off of streets.

So they decided to fill one million sandbags. They planned to use the sandbags to build walls to keep the floodwater out.

1. ThinkSpeakListen

Share one key detail you learned from this text.

Understand the Language of <u>Cause</u> and <u>Effect</u>

Cause		Effect
The National Weather Service predicted that bad flooding would hit Fargo, North Dakota...		**So** elected officials from the federal, state, and city governments met....
They wanted to keep water out of homes and businesses, and off of streets.		**So** they decided to fill one million sandbags. They planned to use the sandbags to build walls to keep the floodwater out.

The National Weather Service was right. In April, the Red River rose. This caused flooding in the area around Fargo. People used the sandbags to build walls. The walls helped keep the water from rushing in. As a result, no homes or businesses were badly damaged. Because the government and citizens worked together, the city of Fargo was safe.

2. ThinkSpeakListen
What were the causes and effects of the plan to protect Fargo from flooding?

Election Day by Nell Wilson

On Election Day, United States' citizens age eighteen and older can vote. They vote in special places called polls.

They vote for candidates—the people running for office....

Voters receive a ballot. The ballot lists the names of the candidates.

Each voter chooses one candidate for each office then casts his or her vote....

Fighting to Vote

Only men age twenty-one or older who owned land could vote in the first presidential election (1788). In most states, only white people could vote....

In 1870, the Fifteenth Amendment to the Constitution was passed. It gave African American men the right to vote....

Women were not allowed to vote at first. Then, in the mid-1800s, they started to fight for this right.... They finally gained the right to vote in 1920.

Young adults ages eighteen to twenty did not get the right to vote until 1971.... Even if you cannot vote now, you can remind people to vote.

3. ThinkSpeakListen

Do you think people under the age of eighteen should be allowed to vote? Think of reasons and evidence to support your opinion.

Robert's Rules of Order

People in businesses, clubs, and schools often work together in groups. Sometimes they hold meetings to discuss ideas and plans…. Imagine a large meeting where everyone is talking at the same time. Not much would get accomplished!… So most groups find it helpful to follow some rules. The rules they most often rely on are *Robert's Rules of Order*….

Henry Robert (1837–1923) was an army officer in the 1800s…. He read many books about how to run meetings. Then he used what he learned to write his own book, called *Robert's Rules of Order*. It was first printed in 1876.

Today, people all over the world still use Henry Robert's book. His rules help people avoid problems and conflicts.

Henry Robert

4. ThinkSpeakListen

Why do you think it is important to have rules for a meeting?

Use Concrete and Abstract Nouns

Example from "Election Day"	Noun	Type
They vote in special places called **polls**.	poll 	concrete
Voters receive a **ballot**.	ballot 	concrete
Young adults ages eighteen to twenty did not get the **right** to vote until 1971.	right	abstract
It is every citizen's right and **responsibility** to vote.	responsibility	abstract

Today, people all over the world still use Henry Robert's book. His rules help people avoid problems and conflicts.

5. ThinkSpeakListen

Imagine that you are voting for the first time. Use the words in the chart above to describe your experience. What would you see? How would you feel?

It Is My Right! by Harper Larios

After the Civil War, Jim Crow laws kept African Americans from enjoying all their rights. Public places were often segregated....

Rosa Parks

On December 1, 1955, Rosa Parks boarded a city bus in Montgomery, Alabama....

The first ten seats of the bus were for white passengers only. Rosa Parks sat behind those seats in a seat for African Americans.

Soon the bus was full. A white man got on. The bus driver told Rosa Parks to give her seat to the man. She politely refused to move, so the bus driver called the police....

6. ThinkSpeakListen

Describe what happened to Rosa Parks on December 1, 1955.

In her autobiography, Parks wrote, "I had no idea when I refused to give up my seat on that Montgomery bus that my small action would help put an end to the segregation laws in the South. I only knew that I was tired of being pushed around...."

Rosa Parks's actions made many people take action, too. Other women called for a boycott of the Montgomery city buses.... They asked people to walk for one day....

Dr. Martin Luther King Jr.

Dr. Martin Luther King Jr., a leader in the African American community, thought the boycott was a good idea. King believed in changing things peacefully.

The one-day boycott was a success.... King became the leader of a group that called for a longer boycott of the city buses. For 381 days, most African Americans refused to ride the Montgomery city buses.

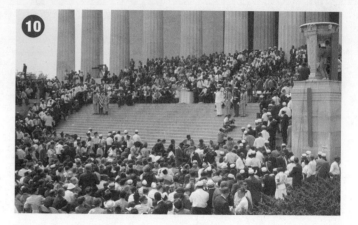

When Martin Luther King Jr. spoke, people listened. He talked about how black Americans and white Americans were treated differently. His words made some people angry.... King continued to speak out for peaceful change....

On August 28, 1963, Dr. King gave one of his most important speeches. Standing in front of the Lincoln Memorial in Washington, D.C., he looked out at 250,000 people....

Dr. King spoke about his dreams: "I have a dream that my four little children will one day live in a nation where they will not be judged by the color of their skin but by the content of their character."

7. ThinkSpeakListen

Compare and contrast the ways Rosa Parks and Martin Luther King Jr. helped to bring an end to segregation in the South.

Understand the Language of <u>Cause</u> and <u>Effect</u>

Cause	Signal Word	Effect
She politely refused to move,	**so**	the bus driver called the police.

Effect	Signal Word	Cause
Rosa Parks was arrested	**because**	she didn't do what the driver told her to do.

Cause	Signal Word	Effect
Rosa Parks's actions	**made**	many people take action, too.

Cause	Signal Word	Effect
His words	**made**	some people angry.

8. ThinkSpeakListen

Use cause and effect language to explain how Rosa Parks and Dr. Martin Luther King Jr. changed segregation laws.

Thomas Paine

Thomas Paine… was a key person in America's fight for independence….

Thomas Paine

In 1776, Paine wrote a pamphlet called *Common Sense*. He explained that it was just common sense to separate from England. He used plain, clear language. Thousands of copies of *Common Sense* were sold. It became what we call today a best seller. Paine's writing swayed many of the undecided.

Thomas Paine is often called the Father of the American Revolution. John Adams said, "Without the pen of the author of *Common Sense*, the sword of George Washington would have been raised in vain."

9. ThinkSpeakListen

How did Thomas Paine help cause the American Revolution?

Writing to Sources

Write a paragraph explaining the actions people took to end segregation laws in the South. Use facts and details from "It Is My Right!" to support your explanation.

Type of writing
Purpose for writing
Source you will use

Sample Paragraph

In the 1950s, many people fought to end segregation. For many years, African Americans did not have the same rights as other Americans. Laws called Jim Crow laws segregated, or separated, them from white Americans. Rosa Parks and Dr. Martin Luther King Jr. were leaders who thought that these laws were unfair. They helped start a boycott to protest these laws. At the same time, Dr. King gave important speeches, led marches, and helped people vote. **As a result** of these actions, segregation laws were changed, and African Americans were given more rights.

A paragraph should include a topic sentence, body sentences, and a closing sentence.

In the 1950s, many people fought to end segregation.

The first sentence of the paragraph should introduce the topic.

For many years, African Americans did not have the same rights as other Americans. Laws called Jim Crow laws segregated, or separated, them from white Americans. Rosa Parks and Dr. Martin Luther King Jr. were leaders who thought that these laws were unfair. They helped start a boycott to protest these laws. At the same time, Dr. King gave important speeches, led marches, and helped people vote.

The sentences in the body of the paragraph should develop and support the topic with facts, definitions, and details.

As a result of these actions, segregation laws were changed, and African Americans were given more rights.

The closing sentence restates the original topic and provides a sense of closure.

Winning the Right to Vote

by T. P. Durban

After the Civil War, all African Americans in the United States were now free. They received the rights of an American citizen. In 1868, the Fourteenth Amendment was added to the U.S. Constitution to say they had those rights.

Some states would not let African American men vote.... Then some states added poll taxes, while others made people pass tests to vote....

By the 1960s, many Americans thought these states were wrong.... Although it was often dangerous, people marched in the streets to demand their right to vote....

The Twenty-Fourth Amendment got rid of poll taxes. Then in 1965, President Johnson signed the Voting Rights Act, which protects the rights of African Americans and others to vote....

Women and the Right to Vote

Lucretia Mott

Elizabeth Cady Stanton

Women had to battle long and hard to win the vote, too.... Lucretia Mott and Elizabeth Cady Stanton were leaders in the cause for women's equality....

Women continued to fight to win the vote, but they didn't always agree on how they should do it. One group wanted to convince states to change their voting laws. Another group thought it would be better to change the U.S. Constitution....

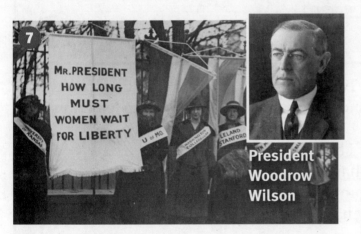

MR. PRESIDENT HOW LONG MUST WOMEN WAIT FOR LIBERTY

President Woodrow Wilson

They picketed in front of the White House.... Finally President Wilson agreed to support their cause.

In 1920, the Nineteenth Amendment became a part of the Constitution. Women had won the right to vote.

10. ThinkSpeakListen

Why is it important for people to fight for their rights?

Understand the Language of <u>Cause</u> and <u>Effect</u>

Other Groups Fought for the Vote	Cause	Effect
Native Americans 	In 1924, all Native Americans became citizens. They now had the right to vote. <u>But because states still controlled voting,</u>	<u>most Native Americans couldn't vote.</u>
Asian Americans 	In 1882, Congress passed a law that stopped Chinese people from coming to the United States. The law also kept people who were from China and other Asian countries from becoming American citizens. <u>Because they weren't citizens,</u>	<u>Asian Americans couldn't vote.</u>
Young Americans 	In 1971, the Twenty-Sixth Amendment was added to the U.S. Constitution. <u>This amendment changed the voting age from twenty-one to eighteen,</u>	<u>so young adults could have a say in elections.</u>

11. ThinkSpeakListen
Compare and contrast the ways African Americans, Native Americans, and Asian Americans were prevented from voting.

Mexican Americans

The United States and Mexico **went** to war in the 1840s. The United States **won** land from Mexico. More than seventy thousand Mexicans living on that land **became** American citizens. Many **were** not allowed to vote.

Things **began** to change after World War II. Mexican American soldiers had **fought**—and died—for the red, white, and blue. When they **came** home, they demanded their rights, including the right to vote.

Form and Use Irregular Verbs

Present Tense	Past Tense
go	went
win	won
become	became
is/are	was (singular); were (plural)
begin	began
fight	fought
come	came

12. ThinkSpeakListen
Choose one of the groups discussed in your reading. Use the irregular verbs in the chart to describe how this group won the right to vote.

One Nation from Many

America's Founding Fathers did not have to go far to find new forms of government. There was a model close by: the Iroquois (EER-uh-kwoi) League of Nations....

The story is told of a man called the Peacemaker, who traveled from nation to nation speaking of peace and unity. He held out one arrow. Alone, it...broke...easily. Then he held out several arrows tied together. The bundle was strong and could not be broken. The Peacemaker showed that unity brought strength.

The nations held a meeting and formed a new, united nation. It was called a League of Nations.... The Founding Fathers used ideas from this League of Nations in their new government. Years later, Congress recognized the League's contribution to the U.S. Constitution.

13. ThinkSpeakListen

How are the Peacemaker's ideas about unity similar to those of the people who organized the Montgomery Bus Boycott?

Understand Subject/Verb Agreement

	Subject Noun	Verb	
	The ballot |___ singular ___| lists		the names of the candidates.
	The ballots |___ plural ___| list		the names of the candidates.
	The woman |___ singular ___| was		not allowed to vote at first.
	Women |___ plural ___| were		not allowed to vote at first.

14. ThinkSpeakListen

Choose one of the people you learned about in your reading. What caused this person to participate in government? What was the effect of his or her participation in government?

How do our actions influence our lives?

Characters face challenges in stories.

My Language Objectives

- Use adjectives and similes to add detail
- Form and use the past and future tenses
- Describe verbs with adverbs
- Write an opinion essay

My Content Objectives

- Build vocabulary related to character action
- Understand how our actions influence our lives

Characters take action in stories.

Characters make decisions in stories.

23

Two Fables *from* Aesop retold by Gare Thompson

The Fox and the Crow

A crow was sitting on a branch of a tree. She had a big piece of cheese in her beak.

A hungry fox came along and watched her. Licking his lips, the fox set about thinking how to get the cheese.

The fox stood right under the crow and looked up. "What a noble bird I see above me!" he said.

"Her beauty is without equal. Her black plumage is as exquisite as a moonless night."

1. ThinkSpeakListen

Why do you think the fox is complimenting the crow?

Use <u>Adjectives</u> and <u>Similes</u> to Add Detail

She had a <u>big</u> piece of cheese in her beak.	
A <u>hungry</u> fox came along and watched her.	
"Her <u>black</u> plumage is as <u>exquisite</u> <u>as a</u> <u>moonless night</u>."	

The crow was flattered. She wanted to show the fox that she could also sing well. She opened her mouth wide and gave a loud caw. Down came the cheese, of course, and the fox snatched it up. Between bites of the cheese, the grinning fox said, "You have a voice, madam, I see, but what you want is wits."

2. ThinkSpeakListen

Look at the pictures in this reading. Describe them using adjectives and similes.

Two Famous Poems

The Ballad of John Henry by Anonymous

When John Henry was a <u>little</u>
  baby,
Just a sittin' on his mama's knee,
He said, "The Big Bend Tunnel
  on that C&O 'Road
Gonna be the death of me,…"

Well John Henry said to the
  Captain,
"I'm gonna take a <u>little</u> trip
  downtown.
Get me a thirty-pound hammer
  with that nine-foot handle
I'll beat your steam drill down,…"

Well John Henry hammered on
  that mountain
Till his hammer was striking fire.
And the very last words that I
  heard that man say was,
"<u>Cool</u> drink of water 'fore I
  die,…"

Well they carried him down to
  the graveyard
And they buried him in the sand.
And every locomotive came a
  roarin' on by
People cried, "There lies a steel-
  drivin' man."

26

The Village Blacksmith by Henry Wadsworth Longfellow

The smith, a <u>mighty</u> man is he,
  With <u>large</u> and <u>sinewy</u> hands;
And the muscles of his <u>brawny</u>
    arms
  Are <u>strong</u> <u>as iron bands</u>.

His hair is <u>crisp</u>, and <u>black</u>, and
    <u>long</u>,
  His face is like the tan;
His brow is <u>wet</u> with honest
    sweat,
  He earns whate'er he can,…

You can hear him swing his
    <u>heavy</u> sledge
  With measured beat and slow,
Like a sexton ringing the village
    bell,
  When the evening sun is low.

And children coming home from
    school
  Look in at the open door;
They love to see the <u>flaming</u>
    forge,
  And hear the bellows roar.

3. Think Speak Listen

Use adjectives and similes to describe the characters of John Henry and the Village Blacksmith.

Geese for the Queen

Once upon a time there were two queens…. One queen was rich… The other was poor, but she gave food to all who were hungry.

One day, three geese landed at the poor queen's feet…. The poor queen scattered some seeds on the ground. "We prefer to eat silver and gold," they said.

"Then you must go see the other queen," replied the poor queen…. The three geese flew off to the rich queen…. She tossed some gold pieces on the ground. As the geese gobbled them up, she dropped a cage on them…. "You may have all the gold you like," the queen said, "but I will not free you."…

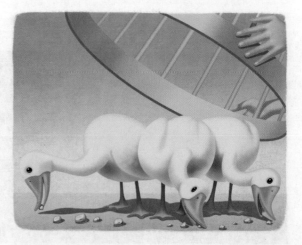

The geese…wanted to return to the poor queen, even if they had to eat seeds. "Our freedom is worth more than gold!" they sighed.

4. ThinkSpeakListen

What lesson did you learn from "Geese for the Queen"?

Use <u>Adjectives</u> and <u>Similes</u> to Add Detail

And the muscles of his <u>brawny</u> arms
    Are <u>strong</u> <u>as iron bands</u>.

You can hear him swing his
<u>heavy</u> sledge…
<u>Like a sexton ringing the village bell.</u>

His face is <u>like the tan.</u>

5. ThinkSpeakListen
Describe a famous person, place, or thing using adjectives and similes.

29

The Tale of King Midas: A Greek Myth retold by Gare Thompson

1

Once long ago, there lived a rich king named Midas.... He loved his daughter, whose name was Marigold. Midas also loved gold.... As time passed, Midas yearned for more and more gold.

2

His dear Marigold would bring him pretty golden buttercups or yellow dandelions from his garden.... But once Marigold was out of sight, Midas would frown....

3

Every day Midas went to his favorite room: the treasury. There he counted his coins.... "I must have more gold," Midas muttered to himself.... "I will take a walk in my garden. Maybe that will make me happy."

4

Midas gazed out over his garden.... His giant sunflowers had turned to face the sun. Their yellow petals shined like gold in the sunlight.... "My flowers are beautiful," sighed Midas, "but they are not real gold." Midas's happiness disappeared like smoke up a chimney.

5

Upon reaching the end of the path, Midas saw a satyr asleep... Satyrs usually stayed in the woods...helping the Greek god Dionysus. This satyr was old and thin, and Midas took pity on him....

6

Midas gently woke the creature and offered him some bread, olives, and water.... So this satyr told Dionysus about Midas's kindness. As is the way of the gods, Dionysus decided to reward Midas.

7

Suddenly a strong wind swirled, and Dionysus appeared in Midas's palace.... His voice was soft and melodious like a flute.... "To reward your kindness, I will grant you one wish."...

8

"I wish that everything I touch will turn to gold," declared Midas.... "I grant your wish, King Midas. Everything you touch will turn to gold." Dionysus's voice echoed in the palace as he disappeared on a gust of wind.

6. ThinkSpeakListen

How would you describe the character of King Midas?

9

Midas began to wander giddily around the palace.... He touched his hairbrush and it turned to gold.... His plates, cups, forks, and spoons turned to gold....

10

He picked up a juicy red apple, but it too turned to inedible gold. "Oh, no!" cried Midas. "If everything I touch turns to gold, I will never be able to eat."...

11

Without thinking, Midas hugged his precious daughter.... Marigold had turned to gold. "Dionysus, please help me," pleaded a weeping Midas.... "Go to the river and wash your hands. Once you do, things will return to normal," said the god.

12

Midas raced to the river and washed his hands until they were as red as bricks. Then he ran back to his palace... Marigold ran down the stairs and hugged her father.... Midas made a decision. He would give away any gold left in the treasury...for all that glitters is not always golden.

7. ThinkSpeakListen

How did King Midas's character traits and actions influence the events of this story?

32

Use <u>Adjectives</u> and <u>Similes</u> to Add Detail

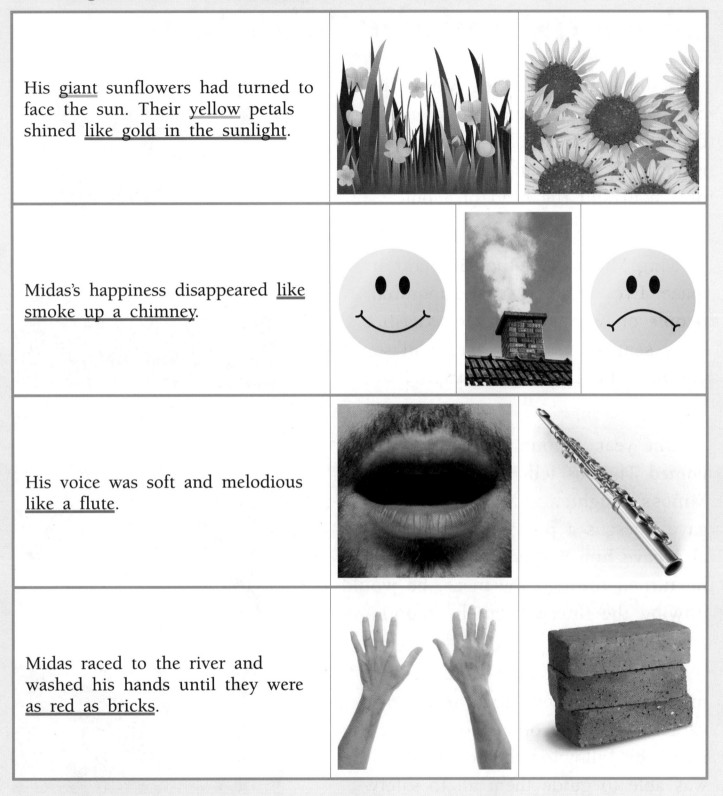

His <u>giant</u> sunflowers had turned to face the sun. Their <u>yellow</u> petals shined <u>like gold in the sunlight</u>.

Midas's happiness disappeared <u>like smoke up a chimney</u>.

His voice was soft and melodious <u>like a flute</u>.

Midas raced to the river and washed his hands until they were <u>as red as bricks</u>.

8. ThinkSpeakListen

Think of a person, place, or thing, and describe it using adjectives and similes.

Theseus and the Minotaur

A long time ago, King Minos lived on the island of Crete… A monster called the Minotaur also lived on the island. The Minotaur had the body of a man and the head of a bull.…

King Minos kept the Minotaur in a maze. Every nine years, he required the people of Athens to make a sacrifice… They sent seven young men and seven young women into the maze.…

One year, a young man from Athens named Theseus fell in love with King Minos's daughter.… Minos's daughter gave Theseus a powerful sword.… She also gave him a spool of thread. While he turned through the maze, he would unwind the thread from the spool.

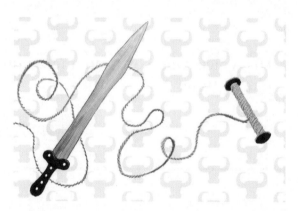

Theseus snuck up behind the monster and sliced off its head. He called out to the others lost in the maze. By following the thread, he was able to guide them all to safety.

9. ThinkSpeakListen
Use adjectives and similes to describe the characters of Theseus and the Minotaur.

Form and Use the Past and Future Tenses

Past Tense

Example from Text	Present Tense	Past Tense
Once long ago, there <u>lived</u> a rich king named Midas.	live	live + d = lived
As time passed, Midas <u>yearned</u> for more and more gold.	yearn	yearn + ed = yearned
Upon reaching the end of the path, Midas <u>saw</u> a satyr asleep.	see	saw (irregular verb)
King Minos <u>kept</u> the Minotaur in a maze.	keep	kept (irregular verb)

Future Tense

Example from Text	Present Tense	Future Tense
"I <u>will take</u> a walk in my garden. Maybe that <u>will make</u> me happy."	take, make	will + take = will take will + make = will make
"To reward your kindness, I <u>will grant</u> you one wish."	grant	will + grant = will grant
"Go to the river and wash your hands. Once you do, things <u>will return</u> to normal," said the god.	return	will + return = will return

10. ThinkSpeakListen

Use past, present, and future tense verbs to describe your week.

Snow White: A Russian Folktale

retold by Lillian Gash

One fine winter's day, Ivan and Marie sat by their cottage window....looking wistfully at a group of merry children making a huge snowman....

After a while Ivan stopped sighing... "Let us go into the garden and play, too." Marie smiled and agreed....

"Let us make a little snow child," she suggested... Soon he was shaping a little body with dainty hands and arms and feet. While he did this, his wife modeled a little head....

He stepped back once more to admire the little figure. As he did so he saw with intense surprise a gentle quiver of its eyelids.... There stood before him a living child!...

11. ThinkSpeakListen

Why did Ivan and Marie decide to go into the garden and play?
How did this decision influence the events of the story?

36

"I am Snow White, your little daughter," exclaimed the figure. She threw her fairy-like arms around Ivan's neck as he bent toward her. Marie, in turn, received a sweet embrace. Then, weeping for joy, they quickly took the girl into their cottage....

Snow White's hair was like fine spun silk. Her eyes were blue as the heavens, and her skin white as snow.... The colder it was, the happier Snow White seemed to be. Her favorite playthings were the glittering icicles that hung from the frosted trees....

In spring, the deep snows melted....as the days grew longer, Snow White lost her joyous spirits and became quiet and sad....instead of playing with the other children, as she had loved to do before, she stayed indoors....

"Snow White! Snow White! Come out and play!" cried a group of her small companions, peeping in through the open door.... "Yes! Go to the woods with your little friends, my darling," said her mother fondly,...

Snow White left the cottage reluctantly, for she would far rather have stayed at home.... Her soft blue eyes dropped tears as she glanced at her father and mother, but they told her to go and play.

A bonfire lit up the marketplace that night. The flames danced high. The sparks flew around in gleaming showers, and the children laughed.

"Look at us, Snow White, and do as we do!" said first one and then another, jumping over the fire. Suddenly they saw that Snow White had vanished.

"Where are you?" cried the children, but there was no reply. Snow White had melted in the heat of the fire, and floated away to the clouds from which she had first come in soft white flakes of snow.

12. ThinkSpeakListen

How are the main characters of "Snow White: A Russian Folktale" similar to the main characters of "The Tale of King Midas: A Greek Myth"?

Describe Verbs with <u>Adverbs</u>

Example from Text	Verb	Adverb
One fine winter's day, Ivan and Marie sat by their cottage window….looking <u>wistfully</u> at a group of merry children making a huge snowman.	looking	wistful + ly = wistfully
Then, weeping for joy, they <u>quickly</u> took the girl into their cottage.	took	quick + ly = quickly
"Yes! Go to the woods with your little friends, my darling," said her mother <u>fondly</u>.	said	fond + ly = fondly
Snow White left the cottage <u>reluctantly</u>, for she would far rather have stayed at home.	left	reluctant + ly = reluctantly
<u>Suddenly</u> they saw that Snow White had vanished.	saw	sudden + ly = suddenly

13. Think**Speak**Listen

Use past tense verbs and adverbs to describe the characters in "Snow White: A Russian Folktale."

Paul Bunyan's Big Thirst

One hot afternoon the giant woodsman Paul Bunyan stretched out across a hillside. The sun made him feel like a log in a woodstove. "I need a cool drink," Paul said.... In the distance, a river wound toward a lakeshore.... He drank that entire river in a heartbeat. Fish flopped about in puddles along the dry riverbed.

Paul was still thirsty, so he scooped up snow from a mountaintop and popped that snowball into his mouth. It felt like a single snowflake landing on Paul's gigantic tongue....

"Now I feel chilly," he said. Paul built a towering campfire on the beach. Folks nearby saw the sky shining with reflected firelight. "Paul must be cold again," they said. "Look at those northern lights!"

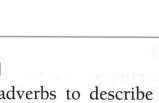

14. ThinkSpeakListen
Use adjectives, similes, and adverbs to describe Paul Bunyan.

Writing to Sources

Is "Snow White: A Russian Folktale" a story you would recommend to your friends? Write a review stating your opinion of the folktale. Support your opinion with reasons from the text. In your conclusion, tell whether you would recommend the story.

Your topic

Purpose for writing

Source you will use

What your concluding statement should include

Sample Essay

I would definitely recommend the story "Snow White: A Russian Folktale" to my friends. The story is beautifully written and illustrated. The language and drawings really help the reader picture what is happening in the story. The story also has an ending that will take readers completely by surprise.

> Your introduction should introduce the topic, state your opinion, and give the reader a brief idea of what you will write about.

The author of "Snow White: A Russian Folktale," Lillian Gash, uses a lot of excellent language to tell the story. She is especially good at using nonliteral language, such as similes. For example, when she describes Snow White, she writes that her hair "was like fine spun silk." She also says that her "eyes were blue as the heavens, and her skin white as snow." I really like this kind of language, since it helps me picture what Snow White looks like while I read. I also liked the illustrations. They were so good that they made me feel like I was reading a graphic novel!

I also really liked the ending of the story. When Snow White started getting sad when the weather got warm, I had a feeling something was going to happen, but I never thought she was going to melt! I thought that was sad, but it was also interesting because it made me think about what Snow White was made of, and how she came alive in the first place.

> Your body paragraphs should provide reasons that support your opinion.

In conclusion, I think "Snow White: A Russian Folktale" is a story every person should read. I think people will find the language and the pictures very entertaining, and the surprise ending will really make them think. I recommend it!

> Your conclusion should restate your opinion, and provide a closing statement.

How do living things adapt to change?

Giraffes use their long necks to reach food in trees.

My Language Objectives

- Identify words that signal context clues
- Understand the language of compare and contrast
- Build research skills
- Distinguish plurals from possessives
- Understand pronoun-antecedent agreement

My Content Objectives

- Build vocabulary related to adaptations
- Understand how living things adapt to change

A lizard's color helps it blend in with its environment.

Some animals live in very cold places.

43

Animal Disguises

by Maria Guerro

All animals have special features that help them stay alive, or survive.

Sometimes, the way they act or behave gives them an advantage. They also have physical features that improve their chances of survival.

For example, animals that hunt for their food are called predators. The animals these predators hunt are called prey.

Both predators and prey have traits that help them hide from one another. How do they do it?

1. ThinkSpeakListen

Why do some animals need "disguises"?

44

Identify Words That Signal Context Clues

Example from Text	Signal Word	Definition
All animals have special features that help them stay alive, **or** survive.	**or**	**survive** = "stay alive"
Sometimes, the way they act **or** behave gives them an advantage.	**or**	**behave** = "act"
For example, animals that hunt for their food are **called** predators.	**called**	**predators** = "animals that hunt for their food"
The animals these predators hunt are **called** prey.	**called**	**prey** = "the animals these predators hunt"
The word *camouflage* **means** "disguise" in French.	**means**	**camouflage** = "disguise"

Many animals have skin or fur that blends into their environment. Their body color matches the colors around them…. This ability to blend into one's surroundings is called camouflage. The word *camouflage* means "disguise" in French. Camouflage is an adaptation—a trait animals are born with that aids in their survival. Camouflage can help prey hide from predators. It can also help a predator remain undetected to sneak up on its prey.

The leaf butterfly relies on camouflage to survive.

2. ThinkSpeakListen
How did the signal words in this chart help you define unfamiliar words?

Animals' Tools for Survival

by Sue Qin

Ducks, like polar bears, use their large webbed feet to move quickly through water.

Ducks and polar bears are born with webbed feet.... This webbing allows the feet to paddle the body through water with ease....

Webbed feet help different animals in different ways. Polar bears use webbed feet to swim faster. Flying frogs use webbed feet to glide through the air.

A claw is a body part at the end of an animal's toe.... Claws have sharp points. Claws have many uses. Like webbed feet, they help animals move faster.

Unlike webbed feet, they also help animals climb and hang in trees.

Whiskers are long, thick hairs.... The whiskers detect movement in air or water. This triggers the nerves to send alert signals to the brain.

Whiskers can help animals move around, or navigate. They also help animals detect danger or locate prey.

A beak is the hard, outer part of a bird's mouth. Some birds, such as herons and pelicans, use their large beaks to catch fish. Others, such as macaws and toucans, use them to reach hard-to-get food.

A long tail helps some animals keep their bodies balanced.... Other animals use their long tails like an extra hand to grab onto things.

On land, in water, or high up in trees, each animal's adapted body part helps it survive.

3. ThinkSpeakListen

Describe the ways that webbed feet, claws, whiskers, beaks, and tails help animals survive.

The Remarkable Teeth of a Shark

Sharks are found in every ocean of the world, far and wide.... Most sharks are carnivores, feeding on fish and other marine animals. And their teeth are perfectly adapted for the job.

Sharks are born with a full set of teeth arranged in rows.... The front row has the largest teeth... When one tooth falls out, a tooth from the next row moves forward to replace it. New teeth form in the back and take its place....

Great white sharks have sharp, wide teeth with saw-like edges. With these teeth, they can catch prey and tear it apart. Mako sharks have thin, sharp teeth like knives, which allow them to hold on to slippery fish. Sharks that roam the ocean floor, like the zebra shark, eat shellfish. Their teeth are thick and flat to crush their prey's shell.

great white shark   mako shark

zebra shark

4. ThinkSpeakListen

Compare the teeth of great white, mako, and zebra sharks. Why are they different?

Understand the Language of <u>Compare</u> and <u>Contrast</u>

Ducks, <u>like</u> polar bears, use their large webbed feet to move quickly through water.

Webbed feet help <u>different</u> animals in <u>different</u> ways. Polar bears use webbed feet to swim faster. Flying frogs use webbed feet to glide through the air.

Claws have sharp points. Claws have many uses. <u>Like</u> webbed feet, they help animals move faster.

<u>Unlike</u> webbed feet, they also help animals climb and hang in trees.

<u>Some</u> birds, such as herons and pelicans, use their large beaks to catch fish. <u>Others</u>, such as macaws and toucans, use them to reach hard-to-get food.

5. Think Speak Listen

Compare and contrast the ways whiskers and tails help some animals survive.

Fur, Skin, Scales, or Feathers

by Anna Miller

Smooth Skins

Amphibians have smooth, wet skin that helps them survive in and out of water.

Frogs are one type of amphibian. Frogs drink and breathe through their skin…. Living near water helps frogs keep their skin moist….

Poison dart frogs can release deadly toxins through their skin. The bright color of this frog's skin is another adaptation that warns predators to stay away—or else.

Salamanders are amphibians, too…. Like poison dart frogs, salamanders can release poison from their skin. Unlike poison dart frogs, salamanders are not brightly colored, but they do have spots on their skin to hide from predators.

Dry Scales

Reptiles are cold-blooded animals. Scales cover their bodies. Scales are made of keratin, the same material in a person's fingernails. Reptiles' scales help them survive in different ways.

Crocodiles are reptiles…. Crocodiles rely on their surroundings to control their body temperature. To warm their bodies, crocodiles lie in the sun. To cool down, crocodiles swim in water….

Lizards are reptiles. An iguana is a kind of lizard…. Iguanas have black, brown, or green scales covering their bodies. The color of their bodies provides camouflage.

Iguanas also depend on their surroundings to control their body temperature. Like crocodiles, iguanas lie in the sun to warm their bodies. However, to cool down, iguanas lie in the shade….

6. ThinkSpeakListen

Use the language of compare and contrast to describe amphibians and reptiles.

Fantastic Feathers

Like reptile scales, feathers are mostly made of keratin. Keratin makes feathers strong and durable. Like scales, feathers protect a bird's body, keeping it warm and dry....

Birds use their feathers in different ways.... Peacocks...use their feathers for defense. When a predator is nearby, the male peacock opens his feathers wide to look bigger.

Macaws live in rain forests.... Their beautiful feathers provide camouflage to hide from predators.

Ducks' feathers serve a special purpose. The air trapped in a duck's downy feathers helps it float on water.

7. ThinkSpeakListen

Use the language of compare and contrast to talk about the features of skin, scales, and feathers.

Understand the Language of Compare and Contrast

Frogs are one type of *amphibian*.... Salamanders are *amphibians*, <u>too</u>.

Crocodiles rely *on their surroundings to control their body temperature*.... Iguanas <u>also</u> depend *on their surroundings to control their body temperature*.

To *cool down*, crocodiles swim in water.... <u>However</u>, to *cool down*, iguanas lie in the shade.

Birds use their *feathers* in <u>different</u> ways....

Peacocks...use their *feathers* for defense.

Macaws live in rain forests.... Their beautiful *feathers* provide camouflage to hide from predators.

The air trapped in a duck's downy *feathers* helps it float on water.

8. ThinkSpeakListen

How does the language of compare and contrast help you better understand the animals described in "Fur, Skin, Scales, or Feathers"?

Caterpillar Self-Defense

Have you ever seen a caterpillar inching along?... Although caterpillars move too slowly to escape, they have ways to protect themselves. Some curl up inside leaves to hide. Others have different means of self-defense.

Camouflage works for some caterpillars. Their coloring helps them blend into the environment. Green caterpillars look like leaves....

Looking dangerous is another way to deter predators. There is a caterpillar that has eye-like spots on its tail. It can puff up its tail to look like a snake and scare birds away.

Some caterpillars really are dangerous to predators because they're poisonous.... The colors warn predators to stay away. It's one more way caterpillars survive.

9. ThinkSpeakListen

Compare and contrast the ways caterpillars use camouflage to the ways the animals discussed in "Animal Disguises" use camouflage.

Building Research Skills

Imagine that you are writing a scene about one of the animals in "Fur, Skin, Scales, or Feathers." Conduct research to answer the following question: What does this animal do when it meets a predator? Read and take notes from two or more sources to answer this question.

Research subject

Research focus

Research goals

Taking Notes

Animal: Salamander

Predators:
- Raccoons
- Squirrels

What does this animal do when it meets a predator?
- Some salamanders secrete a fluid that makes them taste bad.
- Other salamanders squirt poison at their predators.

Source:
Forest Creatures by Abigail Johnson

Animal: Salamander

Predators:
- Chipmunks
- Opossums

What does this animal do when it meets a predator?
- Some nonpoisonous salamanders have spots that make them look like poisonous salamanders.
- When attacked, these salamanders show their spots to scare away predators.

Source:
Animal Survival by Nicholas DeLibero

One Body, Many Adaptations by Judi Black

The Octopus

The octopus lives in the ocean. Its body is very soft and slimy.... Its body covering helps the octopus hide from its predators....

To blend into its surroundings, the octopus has projections sticking out of its skin and special color-changing skin cells....

An octopus's body has several parts that help it survive... An octopus uses its arms for moving, hunting, eating, tasting, and even mating....

The octopus mainly eats shellfish. It uses its mouth to hold down prey and to eat. Its powerful beak-like jaws break open the shells....

10. ThinkSpeakListen

Compare and contrast the adaptations that help sharks and octopuses eat.

The Penguin

Penguins mostly live in very cold places, such as Antarctica.... They spend more than half of their time swimming in icy ocean waters. Predators fly above them and swim below them. So, how does the penguin survive these challenges? Adaptations.

First, the penguin's body covering helps it survive in cold places. Under its skin, the penguin has a layer of fat called blubber. This layer keeps the penguin warm....

Next, the penguin uses camouflage to survive.... The penguin's black back blends in with the dark water. This makes it hard for predators flying above to spot a penguin swimming.

Its white belly blends in with the snow and sunlight. This white coloring makes it hard for predators swimming below to spot them....

The Camel

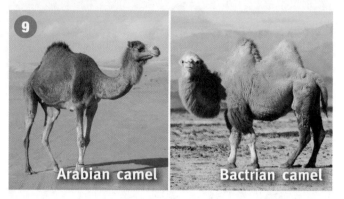
Arabian camel   Bactrian camel

There are two kinds of camels: the Arabian camel…and the Bactrian camel. Both types have many structural adaptations for surviving in deserts.

Camels have thick fur that changes…in winter…a camel's fur grows long to keep its body warm. In summer, a camel's fur sheds so the camel stays cool.…

Camels use camouflage to keep safe, too. Sand covers much of the desert. A camel's brown-colored fur blends in with the sand.…

All camels have humps on their backs.… Why do camels need humps? Water in hot, dry deserts is limited, or scarce. So camels store fat in their humps. A camel's body can change the fat into water when needed.

11. ThinkSpeakListen

What adaptations help penguins and camels survive in their environments?

Distinguish <u>Plurals</u> from <u>Possessives</u>

Example from Text	How It Is Formed	What It Means
<u>**Octopuses**</u> live deep in the ocean.	octopus + es = <u>**octopuses**</u>	more than one octopus
<u>**Penguins**</u> swim safely in cold water.	penguin + s = <u>**penguins**</u>	more than one penguin
<u>**Camels**</u> survive in the hot, dry desert.	camel + s = <u>**camels**</u>	more than one camel
An **octopus's** body has several parts that help it survive.	octopus + ' + s = <u>**octopus's**</u>	**octopus's** body = the body **of** the octopus
The **penguin's** black back blends in with the dark water.	penguin + ' + s = <u>**penguin's**</u>	**penguin's** black back = the black back **of** the penguin
A **camel's** brown-colored fur blends in with the sand.	camel + ' + s = <u>**camel's**</u>	**camel's** brown-colored fur = the brown-colored fur **of** the camel

12. ThinkSpeakListen
Use plurals and possessives, and the language of compare and contrast, to describe the different adaptations of octopuses, penguins, and camels.

How the Chameleon Learned to Change Color

Many years ago, all chameleons were a dull black, brown, or gray. They lived in trees, and their skin matched the tree's bark. One day, a curious chameleon climbed to the top of its tree and looked out at the forest....

Suddenly, a bird swooped out of the sky. It almost caught the chameleon. The chameleon quickly scurried back down the tree....

The chameleon found paint and a brush. Quickly, it painted some green on its back and head, so that it blended in better with the rest of the forest.

After that, birds and other predators had a difficult time seeing the chameleon.

13. ThinkSpeakListen

Make up your own story to describe how one of the animals you read about got its adaptations.

Understand Pronoun-Antecedent Agreement

singular

The <u>octopus</u> mainly eats shellfish. <u>It</u> uses its mouth to hold down prey and to eat.

plural

<u>Penguins</u> mostly live in very cold places, such as Antarctica…. <u>They</u> spend more than half of their time swimming in icy ocean waters.

plural

Many years ago, all <u>chameleons</u> were a dull black, brown, or gray. <u>They</u> lived in trees, and their skin matched the tree's bark.

singular

Suddenly, a <u>bird</u> swooped out of the sky. <u>It</u> almost caught the chameleon.

14. ThinkSpeakListen

Think about the animals you have learned about in your reading. What did they teach you about how living things adapt to change?

Essential Question

What makes people view the same experience in different ways?

My Language Objectives

- Form and use irregular verbs
- Use pronouns to identify point of view
- Understand comparative and superlative adjectives
- Write an opinion essay

My Content Objectives

- Build vocabulary related to point of view
- Understand what makes people view the same experience in different ways

What some people think is fair, other people think is unfair.

What some people think is funny, other people think is mean.

What some people think is strange, other people think is normal.

63

Cinderella's Very Bad Day by Gare Thompson

June 20, 1549, Late Morning

1

My stepsisters have been meaner than a mule today! I woke when the rooster crowed and lit a fire in the downstairs hearth, as usual....

2

Next, I ran to add kindling to the fires in their rooms. I would not have heard the end of it if my stepsisters' large, ugly feet touched a cold floor....

3

My older stepsister demanded soft-boiled eggs. My younger stepsister yelled for medium-boiled eggs. I flew to the kitchen to make their breakfasts....

4

"I can't eat these eggs!" they screamed. "Porridge with berries instead."

FLYING EGG

1. ThinkSpeakListen

Recount the main events of this story.

64

Form and Use Irregular Verbs

Example from "Cinderella's Very Bad Day"	Present Tense	Past Tense
I **woke** when the rooster crowed.	wake	woke
...and **lit** a fire in the downstairs hearth, as usual.	light	lit
Next, I **ran** to add kindling to the fires in their rooms.	run	ran
I would not have **heard** the end of it if my stepsisters' large, ugly feet touched a cold floor.	hear	heard
I **flew** to the kitchen to make their breakfasts.	fly	flew

While picking strawberries, I forgot that they give me a rash. I was soon covered with red blotches. Still, I served the porridge. "Too hot!" cried the older stepsister. "Too cold!" shrieked the younger one. Neither wanted strawberries, so, naturally, they threw them at me. More red blotches.

Meanwhile, dear diary, my stepmother keeps screaming for me. This horrible day will never end.

STRAWBERRIES

2. ThinkSpeakListen
Use these irregular verbs to describe your day.

Cinderella, Too Much for Words

by Gare Thompson

Characters in order of appearance

Stepsister #2
(*Cinderella's Younger Stepsister*)

Stepmother

Scene 2:
Stepsister #2's Bedroom

(*shrieking*) MOTHER! I need you right this instant. NOW!

(*running in*) What disaster has befallen you, my child?

The disaster that has befallen me is Cinderella. She is vile. She is inhumane. She is detestable. She is…

(*smiling*) Good word choices. You might want to share some of your vocabulary with your sister. Now, what has Cinderella done to you?

Well, first she was very late, tardy one might say, and so my room was very cold, freezing one might say, when I woke up.

We must train her to do a better job of serving us.

(*smiling evilly*) Yes, we must. Now, what do you suppose she put on my porridge?

Your least favorite fruit: blueberries?

No, it was strawberries, my *most* favorite! But I saw right through her trick. So I threw the strawberries right at her as if they *were* blueberries.

Well, hopefully the porridge was warm and delectable.

 It was not! It was colder than a snowball wrapped in an icicle.

 Another black mark against Cinderella!

 She is a thorn in our sides and a cross we have to bear.

 Well, settle down under your covers. Rest and compose yourself, as we have to prepare for tonight's ball.

 I will rest, Mother. I hope to dance with the prince all night. Cinderella is not going, is she?

 Of course she is not going. Who would want to dance with *her*?

3. ThinkSpeakListen

"Cinderella's Very Bad Day" and "Cinderella, Too Much for Words" describe the same story events. How do the characters in each story view these events?

Cap o' Rushes

Once upon a time, a rich man sent away his daughter. "You don't love me, Katie!" he said.

"But I love you as fresh meat loves salt," she replied. Katie was sad until she found some rushes along a river. She turned them into a cloak to cover her pretty red dress.…

One night, Katie went to a dance wearing her red dress. Her master's son, Michael, saw her and fell in love.… Michael followed Katie home.… He begged Katie to marry him, and she agreed.

Katie's father went to the wedding. He didn't know the bride was his daughter. Katie had asked the cook to serve meat without salt. It tasted so bad that Katie's father realized he had been wrong about Katie.… They hugged each other and everyone lived happily ever after.

4. ThinkSpeakListen

Why did the "meat without salt" make Katie's father realize he had been wrong?

Use <u>Pronouns</u> to Identify Point of View

Example from "Cinderella's Very Bad Day"

While picking strawberries, **I** forgot that they give **me** a rash. **I** was soon covered with red blotches. Still, **I** served the porridge. "Too hot!" cried the older stepsister. "Too cold!" shrieked the younger one. Neither wanted strawberries, so, naturally, they threw them at **me**. More red blotches.

Meanwhile, dear diary, **my** stepmother keeps screaming for **me**.

Examples from "Cinderella, Too Much For Words"

Stepmother: **We** must train her to do a better job of serving **us**.

Stepsister #2: She is a thorn in **our** sides and a cross **we** have to bear.

First Person Pronouns

	Subject	Object	Possessive
Singular	I	me	my
Plural	we	us	our

5. ThinkSpeakListen

Use first person pronouns to describe your day.

69

Jack and the Beanstalk by the Brothers Grimm

Once upon a time, there lived a poor widow who had an only son named Jack.... they had only their cow to sell....

On his way to market, Jack met a butcher.... The butcher quickly pulled out five curious-looking beans....

He said, "If you plant them overnight, by the next morning they'll grow up and reach the sky. I will trade them for that cow of yours."

"Done!" cried Jack....

His mother, however, was very disappointed and so angry she threw the beans out of the window into the garden...

6. ThinkSpeakListen

Imagine that you are Jack. Create a few sentences using first person pronouns to tell the reader a little bit about yourself and your experiences.

When he woke up the next morning,...beside his window there was a giant beanstalk that stretched up and up as far as he could see...."I'll just see where it leads to," thought Jack....

Finally reaching the top, Jack found himself in a new and beautiful country. He saw a great castle...As Jack drew near to the huge castle, he saw a giant's wife standing at the door.

"If you please, ma'am," said he, "would you kindly give me some breakfast?"...

The giant's wife gave him a good breakfast, but before Jack had half-finished it there came a terrible knock at the front door. It seemed to shake even the thick walls of the castle.

"That is my husband!" said the giantess, in a terrible fright. "We must hide you." No sooner had the giant's wife opened the door than her husband roared out:

"Fee, fi, fo, fum,

I smell the blood of an Englishman..."

"Nonsense!" said his wife. "It's the ox I am making for your dinner that you smell."

So the giant sat down and ate the whole ox.

When he had finished…his wife brought him two full bags of gold, and the giant began to count his money. But he was so sleepy that his head began to nod….

Jack crept out of his hiding spot and snatched up the two bags…. The giant woke up and saw Jack running out. He dashed after Jack…. Jack climbed down the beanstalk….

Upon reaching the ground, Jack cut the beanstalk in two. Down came the giant with a terrible crash! And that was the end of him.

7. ThinkSpeakListen

How do you think the giant's wife would feel about the events of this story?

Form and Use Irregular Verbs

Example from "Jack and the Beanstalk"	Present Tense	Past Tense
Once upon a time, there lived a poor widow who **had** an only son named Jack.	have	had
He **said**, "If you plant them overnight, by the next morning they'll grow up and reach the sky. I will trade them for that cow of yours."	say	said
His mother, however, was very disappointed and so angry she **threw** the beans out of the window into the garden.	throw	threw
"I'll just see where it leads to," **thought** Jack.	think	thought
Finally reaching the top, Jack **found** himself in a new and beautiful country.	find	found
As Jack **drew** near to the huge castle, he saw a giant's wife standing at the door.	draw	drew
Upon reaching the ground, Jack **cut** the beanstalk in two.	cut	cut

8. ThinkSpeakListen
Choose four of these irregular verbs, and use them to describe an experience.

The Giant's Complaint

I'm the giant and I'm here to complain about how the fairy tales always make me out to be a bad guy. What did I do that was so terrible?…

Did I ever blow your house down? No! Gobble up your sweet old grandma? No! I'm not a wolf! In fact, I'm as gentle as a lamb.

That tale about Jack and his beanstalk is a bunch of hooey. The true story is that we were nice to the little guy. My wife fed him and treated him as a guest. But instead of being grateful, Jack stole a bag of gold from us.…

If someone stole your gold, wouldn't you try to catch him? Of course you would.… But unfortunately, I wasn't able to catch Jack.…

Even worse, at the end of the story, Jack is the one who lives happily ever after, not me. Well, I'm fed up!

9. Think Speak Listen

How is the giant's point of view different from that of the narrator of "Jack and the Beanstalk"?

Use <u>Pronouns</u> to Identify Point of View

Examples from "Jack and the Beanstalk"

Once upon a time, there lived a poor widow who had an only son named Jack. Times were hard. Most of **<u>their</u>** furniture had been sold to buy bread. Now **<u>they</u>** had only **<u>their</u>** cow to sell.

When **<u>he</u>** woke up the next morning,…beside **<u>his</u>** window there was a giant beanstalk that stretched up and up as far as **<u>he</u>** could see, into the sky. **<u>He</u>** went outside to get a better look.

Third Person Pronouns

		Subject	Object	Possessive
Singular		he	him	his
		she	her	her
Plural		they	them	their

10. ThinkSpeakListen

Recount the details of "Cinderella's Very Bad Day" using third person pronouns.

The True Jack? by Gare Thompson

Cast of Characters

Host

Mom
(*Jack's Mother*)

Giant

Setting

A castle in the late 1600s.

 Mom—may I call you Mom?—tell us all what Jack was like as a child.

 Oh, he was a sweet, happy child. (*pauses*) But he could never sit still. A regular jumping bean. I had to watch him like a hawk. He would run about and leap off trees without a thought....

 So—Jack was impulsive?

Oh my, yes. Many's the time I wished I had a leash for him. I had to keep an eye on him 24/7....

 Now, Mom, I understand you were upset when Jack came home with those beans.

I was tied to a fit. I mean fit to be tied. What a foolish boy. I was sure the butcher had taken advantage of Jack....

 Let's sum up your point of view. Jack is impulsive and acts before he thinks.

 Yes, but he's a good boy....

11. ThinkSpeakListen

How does this interview add to what you know about the character of Jack? Does it change your opinion of him? If so, how?

Well, let's see what others have to say about Jack. Make room, please, for Mr. Giant.

 Coming through! *Ouch!* You need to make the ceilings higher here.

 Now, Giant, what is your point of view about Jack?

 I have a big point of view about that boy. After all, I am a giant. I have the biggest point of view.

 You're big and you have a big point of view. Tell us what it is, please.

 I think Jack is small. He is smaller than other boys I've e't, I mean met. However, he is the biggest thief.

 My son is a good boy.

He is a big thief. Jack stole my gold, my hen, and my harp....

 So you think Jack is a thief. What else do you have to say about him?

 Jack is mean. He is meaner than an angry snake. He is the meanest lad in the land.

 Jack is a thief, but how is he mean?

 He chopped the beanstalk down while I was on it. I'm lucky I didn't die.

We all thought you did die.

You thought wrong. I got a broken leg, and the town got a hole in the ground that is now a fishpond. But I'm alive. No thanks to that mean thief, Jack.

 Thank you, Giant, for that point of view. (*to audience*) What is your point of view about Jack? Is he lucky? A good boy? Mean? Greedy? Is he impulsive? Kind and smart? Selfish? Or is he something else entirely? You decide.

12. ThinkSpeakListen

How does the Giant's point of view on Jack differ from that of Jack's Mom? Which point of view do you most agree with?

Understand <u>Comparative</u> and <u>Superlative</u> Adjectives

Example from "The True Jack?"

I think Jack is **small**. He is **<u>smaller</u>** than other boys I've e't, I mean met. However, he is the **<u>biggest</u>** thief.

Jack is **mean**. He is **<u>meaner</u>** than an angry snake. He is the **<u>meanest</u>** lad in the land.

I have a **big** point of view about that boy. After all, I am a giant. I have the **<u>biggest</u>** point of view.

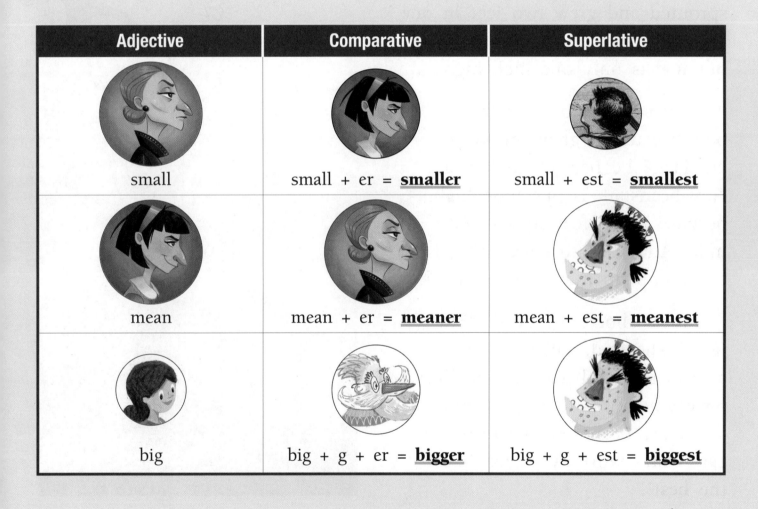

Adjective	Comparative	Superlative
small	small + er = **<u>smaller</u>**	small + est = **<u>smallest</u>**
mean	mean + er = **<u>meaner</u>**	mean + est = **<u>meanest</u>**
big	big + g + er = **<u>bigger</u>**	big + g + est = **<u>biggest</u>**

13. Think Speak Listen

Compare the characters from the Cinderella and Jack and the Beanstalk stories you read. Make sure to include comparative and superlative adjectives in your comparisons.

The Beanstalk Experiment

Jack and his friend Rayna conducted a science experiment. Jack planted one of the beans that he found in the giant's house. Meanwhile, Rayna planted a regular green bean.

A week later, Jack's bean sprouted and grew two feet in one night. Rayna's bean sprouted too, but it was only one inch high....

Jack said his bean is the best because it grew the tallest. "In fact," he boasted to Rayna, "my beanstalk is one mile high, because 5,280 feet equals one mile. And it is so sturdy that I can climb up it high into the sky."

Rayna shook her head. "But Jack," she said, "all you have is a beanstalk and leaves. You don't have any beans to eat!... Pretty soon, my beans will be ready to eat. That's why my beanstalk is the best!"

14. ThinkSpeakListen

Whose beanstalk is the best? Do you agree with Jack, or do you agree with Rayna? Support your opinion with specific reasons.

Writing to Sources

In the play "The True Jack?," each character shares his or her opinion of Jack, the main character in "Jack and the Beanstalk." Which character's point of view do you most agree with? State your opinion, and support it using details from both texts.

Sources for writing

Writing focus

Writing goal

Sample Essay

In "The True Jack?," different characters from "Jack and the Beanstalk" talk about their opinions of Jack. Some characters think he is a good boy. Others, like the giant, think he is "the meanest lad in the land." I agree with the giant. The giant may be mean, but Jack is definitely meaner.

Your introduction should introduce the topic, state your opinion, and give the reader a brief idea of what you will write about.

In "Jack and the Beanstalk," we learn that Jack and his mother are the poorest people in the land. Jack, however, decides to trade the cow to a butcher for some beans. I think it was wrong for Jack to disobey his mother. After all, what if the beans turned out to be just normal beans? Then Jack would have given away all they had for nothing. Luckily for Jack, the beans turned out to be magical beans that grew into a giant beanstalk.

After he climbs the beanstalk, Jack meets a giantess, who kindly gives him breakfast. She even hides him when the giant comes home. She could not have been kinder. How does Jack repay her? He steals the giant's gold! Then, Jack cuts down the beanstalk while the giant is still on it. According to "Jack and the Beanstalk," this fall killed the giant, but according to "The True Jack?," the fall only broke his leg. Either way, I think it was wrong for Jack to hurt the giantess's husband after she had been so kind. He should have just walked away without taking the gold.

Your body paragraphs should provide reasons that support your opinion.

All of these reasons show why the giant was right about Jack in "The True Jack?" Jack might be brave, but he is also the sneakiest and rudest character in the story. I think more people should consider the giant's point of view.

Your conclusion should restate your opinion, and provide a closing statement.

Essential Question

What is the value of innovation?

technology of the past

My Language Objectives

- Understand sequential language
- Write a historical narrative
- Form and use irregular verbs
- Identify and understand multiple text structures
- Understand how demonstrative pronouns and adjectives connect ideas in a text

My Content Objectives

- Build vocabulary related to innovation
- Understand the value of innovation

technology of today

technology of the future

Alexander Graham Bell: "It Talks!" by Kathy Furgang

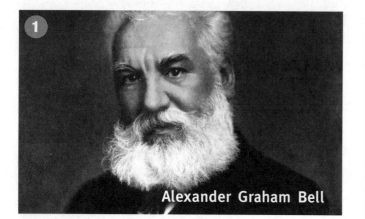

Alexander Graham Bell

Telephones have connected people to one another since the late 1800s. Alexander Graham Bell invented this important communication tool....

Bell dreamed that people would one day "talk with electricity." At the time, people could only send telegraphs. These were coded messages sent over wires using a system of clicks and blips....

After many tries, Bell finally succeeded. On March 10, 1876, a call reached his assistant in the next room...Bell had achieved his goal....

Bell brought his telephone to the 1876 World's Fair in Philadelphia, Pennsylvania. He called it an "electrical speech machine." People were amazed at Bell's work.

1. ThinkSpeakListen

How is the telephone an improvement over the telegraph?

Understand Sequential Language

Bell dreamed that people would one day "talk with electricity." At the time, people could only send telegraphs.

After many tries, Bell finally succeeded. On March 10, 1876, a call reached his assistant in the next room.

Bell brought his telephone to the 1876 World's Fair in Philadelphia, Pennsylvania.

The leader of Brazil, Emperor Pedro II, was at the fair. When he heard sound through the telephone wire, he dropped the phone. "It talks!" he cried out.

Bell's invention was revolutionary. **In 1877**, he established the Bell Telephone Company. **Three years later** there were more than 130,000 phones in American homes. Bell's invention paved the way for how we communicate today.

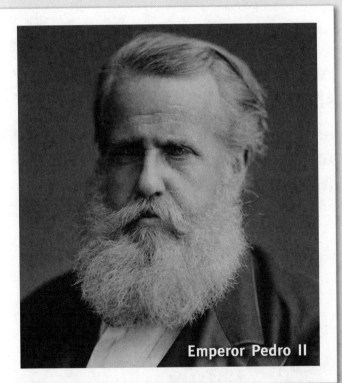

Emperor Pedro II

2. ThinkSpeakListen

Explain what you think the author means when she writes that "Bell's invention paved the way for how we communicate today."

From Telephone to FaceTime by Caleb Adams

Rutherford B. Hayes

President Rutherford B. Hayes, nineteenth president of the United States, tested the telephone back in 1876. He had one put into the White House a year later. However, he had this to say about the telephone: "An amazing invention, but who would ever want to use one?"

1 At first, the telephone was a strange new idea to the world.... Once people saw how useful a telephone could be, the demand for phones went up sharply.

2 By 1900, Bell's company had almost 600,000 phones in use. That number increased to 6 million by 1910....

3 For almost a century, telephone signals could only be sent along cables and into the walls of buildings. Cable phones are called "landlines."

4 But another important discovery came along in 1973: the world's first cell phone. People could now carry a phone down the street!

5

Cellular phone technology is different from landline technology. Signals go through the air instead of through wires.... But the first cell phones were big and cost a lot of money, too....

6

Cell phones did not get small enough to fit into people's pockets until around 2000. Once that happened, more and more people bought them.

7

Many phones became "smarter," too. These "smartphones" can do a lot more than make calls. They work like computers....

8

Now video calls can be made from a cell phone. People can send photos and written messages with cell phones, too. They can surf the Internet.

3. ThinkSpeakListen

Based on what you read in "From Telephone to FaceTime," make predictions about how we will communicate in the future.

The Longest Wire

Before the invention of the telephone (1876), the telegraph (1844) let people communicate across great distances.... Communication across the Atlantic Ocean was a different story.... Businessman Cyrus Field imagined a time when a message from North America would reach Europe in just one day!...

Cyrus Field

Many thought it wasn't possible. Field was sure it was. Inventors made a strong cable that could carry the signals....

In 1857, two ships set out to lay the wire. The cable snapped 200 miles from shore. Field tried again in June of 1858. This time, a huge storm nearly sank one of the ships. Plus, the cable broke again. That same summer, Field tried yet again. This time everything worked. Field himself rowed ashore to make the final connection. America and Europe were joined! People celebrated with parties and fireworks.

4. ThinkSpeakListen

Why do you think the people of Cyrus Field's time thought it would be impossible to send a message from North America to Europe in just one day?

Writing to Sources

Pretend you are Alexander Graham Bell. Write two paragraphs in which you describe your meetings with Emperor Pedro II and President Hayes. Make sure your narrative includes facts and details from "Alexander Graham Bell: 'It Talks!'" and "From Telephone to FaceTime."

Narrator

Situation

Source

Sample Essay

When I presented my new electrical speech machine at the 1876 World's Fair in Philadelphia, it was one of the proudest moments of my life. I knew that my invention would change people's lives, but I was surprised by the reaction. People were amazed! Pedro II, the emperor of Brazil, attended the fair and tried the machine. When he heard sound coming out of it, he was very surprised. He shouted, "It talks!" and dropped it on the floor. Fortunately, it was not broken, and everyone had a good laugh.

The introduction introduces the narrator and establishes the situation of the story.

Unlike Pedro II, President Hayes was not very excited about my invention. After the World's Fair, I visited Washington, D.C. to show it to him. My assistant came with me because we are planning to install one of these electrical speech machines in the White House next year. When the president heard a voice coming through the machine, he said, "An amazing invention, but who would ever want to use one?" I disagree with the president. I predict that within a few years, my speech machine will be used in over 100,000 American homes. I believe that it will completely change the way people communicate.

The next paragraph uses the language of sequence, dialogue, and description to develop the story.

The last few sentences provide a sense of closure.

Thomas Edison: "It Sings!" by Elizabeth Michaels

In 1876, Edison attended the Centennial Exhibition world's fair in Philadelphia, Pennsylvania. He displayed one of his automatic telegraph machines. It could send messages at high speeds....

While at the fair, Edison was inspired by what he saw.... Edison was especially curious about a device on display called a "telephone."...

In 1877, Edison worked on a way to improve Bell's telephone. He made it possible for voices to sound louder and clearer over the telephone wires....

As a result of his experiments, Edison ended up with a new kind of sound machine. He invented the first phonograph. He found a way to record sound on a cylinder coated with tinfoil.

5. Think Speak Listen

Using the language of sequence, describe how Thomas Edison developed the first phonograph.

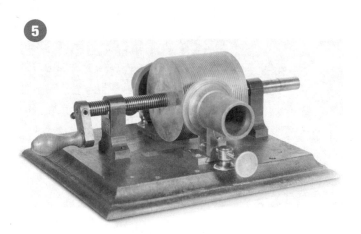

5

The machine had one needle for recording sound. It also had a needle for playing back sounds. As sounds vibrated, the needle pressed into the cylinder in the same pattern....

6

Edison knew this invention was important. He saw the many ways it could help people communicate. People could record letters on the cylinders instead of writing them down on paper....

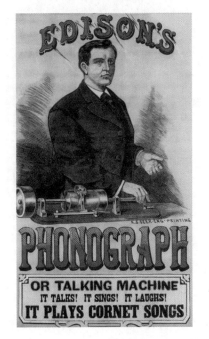

7

EDISON'S PHONOGRAPH

OR TALKING MACHINE
IT TALKS! IT SINGS! IT LAUGHS!
IT PLAYS CORNET SONGS

Edison started a company that sold phonographs and cylinders. People bought cylinders with their favorite music on it....

8

Edison's fame increased. In 1878 he was invited to the White House to demonstrate the phonograph to President Rutherford B. Hayes. Edison was nicknamed the "Wizard of Menlo Park" by a newspaper reporter....

Edison still brimmed with great ideas. For two years, he and the scientists in his lab worked hard on a new project. They wanted to develop a lightbulb that used less electricity than other bulbs and could burn much longer....

In 1879, they produced a lightbulb that glowed for more than fourteen hours, longer than any other lightbulb. Until that time, typical bulbs lasted only a few minutes.

Edison eventually produced bulbs that could glow for over 1,500 hours. They looked very much like the lightbulbs we see in our homes today.

By the age of eighty-three, Thomas Edison had obtained 1,093 patents for his inventions. His work improved the way in which we communicate every day.

6. ThinkSpeakListen

Describe how Thomas Edison's inventions have improved the way we communicate with one another.

Form and Use Irregular Verbs

Example from "Thomas Edison: 'It Sings!'"	Present Tense	Past Tense
He **made** it possible for voices to sound louder and clearer over the telephone wires.	make	made
Edison **knew** this invention was important.	know	knew
Edison started a company that **sold** phonographs and cylinders.	sell	sold
People **bought** cylinders with their favorite music on it.	buy	bought
They wanted to develop a lightbulb that used less electricity than other bulbs and **could** burn much longer.	can	could

7. ThinkSpeakListen
Use the irregular verbs above to describe the invention of the telephone and how it became popular.

George Eastman and the Kodak Camera

In 1878, George Eastman, age twenty-four, worked as a bank clerk in Rochester, New York. He was planning a trip to a Caribbean island. His coworkers suggested that he take pictures.

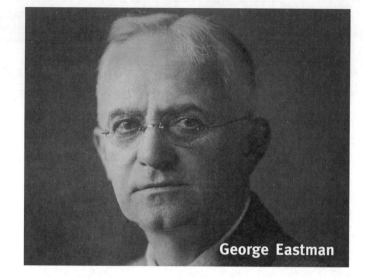

George Eastman

At that time, taking pictures wasn't easy.... Eastman wanted to make the process simpler.... He wanted to invent a smaller, portable camera that the general public could use.... In 1888, his invention was ready. The first Kodak cameras appeared in stores.

The Kodak camera became one of the most popular inventions of all time.... As one of the "fathers of photography," George Eastman was the very picture of success!

8. ThinkSpeakListen

How was the invention of the Kodak camera similar to the invention of the telephone?

94

Identify and Understand Multiple Text Structures: Sequence, Cause and Effect, Compare and Contrast

Example from Text
In 1877, Edison worked on a way to improve Bell's telephone. He made it possible for voices to sound louder and clearer over the telephone wires.
As a result of his experiments, Edison ended up with a new kind of sound machine.
The machine had one needle for recording sound. It also had a needle for playing back sounds. As sounds vibrated, the needle pressed into the cylinder in the same pattern.
In 1879, they produced a lightbulb that glowed for more than fourteen hours, longer than any other lightbulb.
Edison eventually produced bulbs that could glow for over 1,500 hours. They looked very much like the lightbulbs we see in our homes today.
By the age of eighty-three, Thomas Edison had obtained 1,093 patents for his inventions. His work improved the way in which we communicate every day.

9. ThinkSpeakListen

Use the language of sequence, cause and effect, and compare and contrast to describe the invention of the telephone and phonograph.

From Phonograph to Playlist by Ben Foster

The word *phonograph* means "writing sound" in Greek…. The early machine recorded sounds with a needle onto a cylinder covered in foil…. Thomas Edison developed the phonograph in 1877.

While Edison worked on the lightbulb, other inventors… improved Edison's phonograph. They replaced foil cylinders with cylinders made of wax….

Once Edison finished his work on the lightbulb, he got back to improving the phonograph. First, he switched to wax cylinders.

He used a thicker, harder wax. This made it possible to play the cylinder over 100 times. Then, Edison figured out a way to produce a lot of cylinders at one time….

10. ThinkSpeakListen
Explain how Edison and other inventors improved the phonograph.

5

In the late 1880s, Emile Berliner, another inventor, developed a new type of record. Instead of cylinders, he used flat discs to record sound.... The quality of the sound was much better on discs than on the wax cylinders....

6

People played their discs on a new device called a gramophone.... People bought gramophones and phonographs to play all the recordings now available to them.... It was the beginning of the recording business we know today....

7

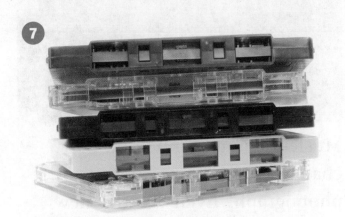

Compact cassettes became popular with music lovers in the 1970s. These cassettes recorded sounds on a long magnetic strip. Soon they outsold records.

8

The 1979 introduction of the portable cassette player changed the music-listening experience even more. People could carry this small stereo system in a pocket....

9

The first compact disc, or CD, was released in 1982. A CD is a small plastic disc that stores music and other digital information.... The discs were small and could hold more music than a record....

10

Once personal computers and the Internet became commonplace, music could be stored on very small digital files.... People could now store hundreds of songs on a computer....

11

The Apple iPod, released in 2001, became a popular personal media player. By the fall of 2010, almost 275 million iPods had been sold worldwide....

12

Music-playing technology has changed a lot since Edison's first phonograph. Even so, the new devices do basically the same thing as the old ones: they play your favorite music!

11. ThinkSpeakListen

Think of the devices you use to listen to music today. What are some ways you would like to improve these devices?

Understand How Demonstrative Pronouns and Adjectives Connect Ideas in a Text

Examples from "From Phonograph to Playlist"	Demonstrative Pronoun	Antecedent
He used a thicker, harder <u>wax</u>. <u>This</u> made it possible to play the cylinder over 100 times.	this	wax
They replaced foil cylinders with <u>cylinders</u> made of wax. <u>These</u> made the sound much clearer.	these	cylinders

Examples from "From Phonograph to Playlist"	Demonstrative Adjective	Noun It Describes
The 1979 introduction of <u>the portable cassette player</u> changed the music-listening experience even more. People could carry <u>this small stereo system</u> in a pocket.	this	portable cassette player/stereo system
<u>Compact cassettes</u> became popular with music lovers in the 1970s. <u>These cassettes</u> recorded sounds on a long magnetic strip.	these	cassettes

12. ThinkSpeakListen

Use demonstrative pronouns and adjectives to help you describe how the telephone and the phonograph changed people's lives.

From Snapshots to Selfies

Many people today enjoy sharing pictures with friends. Some people like using old-style cameras to capture images. Others rely on their cell phones and digital devices....

Early photographers carried glass plates and chemicals along with huge cameras. George Eastman introduced the smaller, simpler Kodak camera in 1888.... Eastman made taking snapshots as easy as pressing a button!

People relied on experts to develop their film and print pictures. Then they taped or pasted their photos into albums or scrapbooks. Families gathered together and shared memories while looking at the pictures....

Today, taking pictures is easier than ever. Some apps can change the look of your photos.... Many modern cameras also have a setting for "selfies," or self-portraits. These days, the photographer is often the subject!

13. ThinkSpeakListen

Compare the ways people used to take and share photographs to the way they take and share photographs today.

Understand Sequential Language

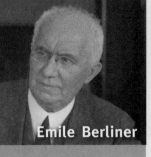

Emile Berliner

Once Edison finished his work on the lightbulb, he got back to improving the phonograph.

First, he switched to wax cylinders.

Then, Edison figured out a way to produce a lot of cylinders at one time.

In the late 1880s, Emile Berliner, another inventor, developed a new type of record.

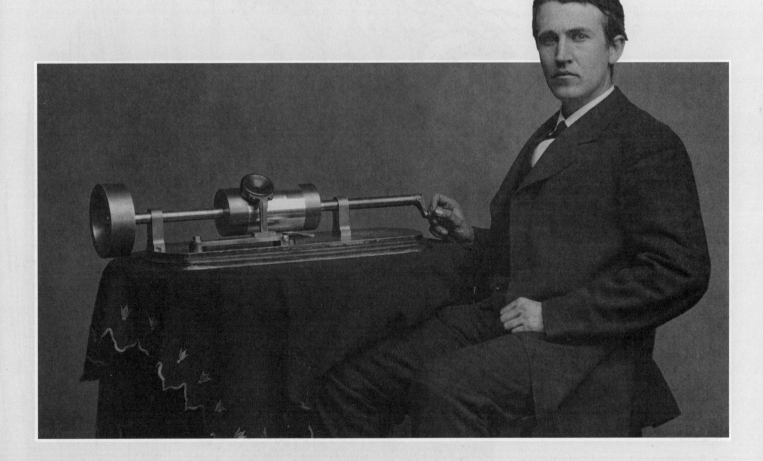

14. Think Speak Listen

Use the language of sequence to describe the ways the telephone, phonograph, and Kodak camera improved people's lives.

Essential Question

What helps us solve problems?

How do we deal with difficult situations?

My Language Objectives

- Use adjectives and adverbs to add details
- Use conjunctions to connect ideas
- Link pronouns and antecedents
- Use prepositional phrases to add detail
- Paraphrase to avoid plagiarism

My Content Objectives

- Build vocabulary related to solving problems
- Understand what helps us solve problems

How do we resolve conflicts?

How do we overcome challenges?

103

The Fox and the Geese by the Brothers Grimm

A hungry fox came to a meadow. He saw a flock of fine fat geese. The fox smiled and licked his lips....

"I have come at the right time. You are sitting together quite beautifully. I can eat you up one after the other."

The geese cackled with terror.... they begged piteously for their lives.... At length, one brave goose took heart and said..."Please allow us one more song. That way we may die happy and free...."

"That is a reasonable request," said the fox. "Sing away. I will not eat you until you are done...."

1. ThinkSpeakListen

Explain the problem the geese face in this story.

Use <u>Adjectives</u> and <u>Adverbs</u> to Add Details

Example from Text

A <u>hungry</u> fox came to a meadow.	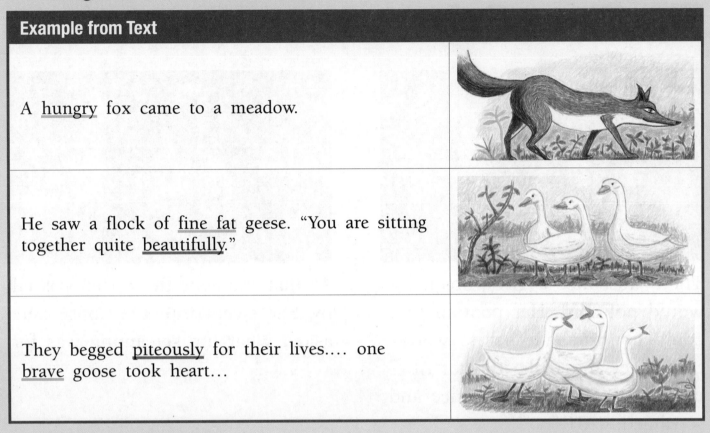
He saw a flock of <u>fine fat</u> geese. "You are sitting together quite <u>beautifully</u>."	
They begged <u>piteously</u> for their lives…. one <u>brave</u> goose took heart…	

When the geese have finished their singing, the story shall be continued further. But at present they are still singing without stopping. And that fox is still very, very hungry.

2. Think Speak Listen
Use adjectives and adverbs to describe the characters in this story.

The Three Spinsters by the Brothers Grimm

There was once a girl who just would not spin. Her poor mother could not persuade her to work the wheel and make thread. At last, the mother lost patience and screamed, "AH!"…

At that moment the queen passed by. She swept into the house and asked what the screaming was for.

The woman was ashamed to tell of her daughter's poor spinning ability, so she said, "I cannot stop her from spinning.…"

The queen thought, then said… "Let me take your daughter to the castle. I have plenty of flax."…

At the castle, the queen showed the girl three rooms filled with the finest flax.

"Now spin and spin and when you have spun a ton," said the queen, "you shall marry my eldest son."…

While staring out the window instead of spinning, the forlorn girl saw three women passing by.... "Hey, there!" called out the girl.... "I am up here spinning. Want to help?" The three women smiled, for they indeed loved to spin.

The women conferred then said, "We will finish your spinning. But you must call us your cousins and invite us to your wedding."

"Done!" cried the girl. "Please spin now."...

The three spinsters spun all day long. Heaps of flax filled three rooms. As the three spinsters took their leave, they said, "Do not forget your promise ... cousin."...

On the day of the wedding feast, in sauntered the three spinsters, delighted to be at the affair. "Dear cousins, welcome," said the bride with a knowing nod and wink.

3. ThinkSpeakListen

Why do you think the woman did not want to admit that her daughter could not spin?

The Incredible Goose

People have raised geese for centuries. They're prized for their meat and their large eggs. But geese are also useful in other ways. Like goats or sheep, they help farmers by eating weeds....

Geese spend most of their lives in flocks, except when they are nesting. The flock's honking scares away predators like wolves or foxes. A male and female goose mate for life. The father helps the mother raise the baby geese, or goslings.

Geese eat grains, grass, and other plants. But how does a goose chew without teeth? It swallows small stones and pebbles. The pebbles stay in the goose's stomach, helping to grind the food as it passes through.

4. ThinkSpeakListen

Explain how geese eat and protect themselves from predators.

Use Conjunctions to Connect Ideas

	Conjunction	
At last, the mother lost patience. The mother screamed, "AH!"	**and**	At last, the mother lost patience **and** screamed, "AH!"
She swept into the house. She asked what the screaming was for.	**and**	She swept into the house **and** asked what the screaming was for.
The woman was ashamed to tell of her daughter's poor spinning ability. She said, "I cannot stop her from spinning."	**so**	The woman was ashamed to tell of her daughter's poor spinning ability, **so** she said, "I cannot stop her from spinning…"
The three women smiled. They indeed loved to spin.	**for**	The three women smiled, **for** they indeed loved to spin.

5. ThinkSpeakListen

Explain how the girl was able to solve the problem she faced in "The Three Spinsters." Make sure to use conjunctions to help you connect and condense your ideas.

Doctor Knowall by the Brothers Grimm

There was once upon a time a poor peasant called Crabb.... He sold his wood to a kind doctor, who invited Crabb into his house so he could pay him.

As the doctor counted out the coins, Crabb noticed the beautiful table filled with fine food...Soon his heart desired what the doctor had...

Gathering up his courage, Crabb inquired, "Might I become a doctor?"...

"Here is what you must do," said the doctor. "You must do three things."

The doctor told Crabb that first he must buy an ABC book.... The second thing to do was to...buy some fine clothes and medicine. The third thing was to have a large, fancy sign painted with the words: "I Am Doctor Knowall."...

6. ThinkSpeakListen

What is your opinion of the advice the doctor gave to Crabb?

110

Crabb immediately did all that the good doctor told him to do. Soon, people came to "Doctor Knowall." After a while, Crabb had many people seeking his advice.

One day, a lord appeared. Now the rich and powerful lord had some money stolen from him. The lord had heard about Doctor Knowall.

The lord assumed with a name like Knowall, the doctor could solve his mystery....

"Are you Doctor Knowall?" the lord demanded. Crabb nodded meekly. "Then you must come with me," commanded the lord.

"I will go but my wife, Grete, must come, too," said Crabb....

Entering the nobleman's castle, they saw a large table upon which were all kinds of plates and goblets that sparkled and shone....

The lord bellowed and the first servant came with a dish of delicate fare. Crabb nudged his wife and said, "Grete, that is the first."

Now what Crabb meant was that he was the servant who brought the first dish, but the servant thought that Crabb meant that he was the first thief—which he actually was—and he was terrified.

So the servant ran back to the kitchen and called to his comrades, "That doctor knows all, and we shall fare ill. We will be caught! He said I was the first."…

Hearing this, the servant-thieves made a sign to the doctor that they wished him to step outside, where they confessed that they had stolen the money.…

Then Crabb showed the lord where the money was, but did not say who had stolen it.… Word of this good doctor's deeds spread and he became a rich, renowned man.

7. ThinkSpeakListen

Why do you think Crabb decided not to say who had stolen the money?

Link Pronouns and Antecedents

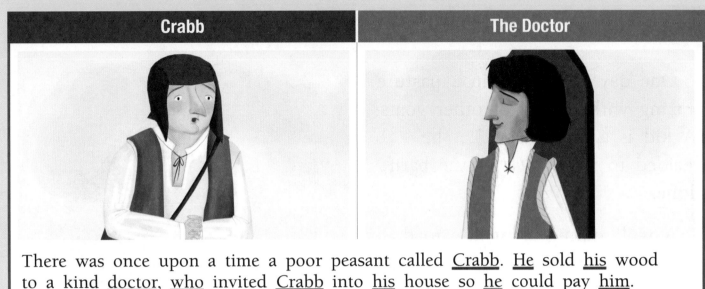

Crabb

The Doctor

There was once upon a time a poor peasant called <u>Crabb</u>. <u>He</u> sold <u>his</u> wood to a kind <u>doctor</u>, <u>who</u> invited <u>Crabb</u> into <u>his</u> house so <u>he</u> could pay <u>him</u>.

Doctor Knowall

The Servant-Thieves

Hearing this, the <u>servant-thieves</u> made a sign to the <u>doctor</u> that <u>they</u> wished <u>him</u> to step outside, where <u>they</u> confessed that <u>they</u> had stolen the money.

8. ThinkSpeakListen

Summarize how Crabb became "a rich, renowned man." Make sure to use correct pronoun-antecedent agreement in your summary.

The Kid and the Wolf

One day a kid was in a pasture, grazing with a herd of other goats. (A kid is a young goat.)... he decided to walk back to the barn alone.

A wolf hiding along the road jumped out and snarled. The kid cried out in fear...."I know, my dear wolf, that I must be your prey, but before I die, I have a favor to ask. Would you play me a tune on your pipe so that I can dance?"

The wolf was flattered and so agreed.... The high sound of the pipe was heard by the farmer's dogs. They quickly raced out of the barnyard and up the road to save the young goat.

The wolf ran away and the kid, wiser now, never left the pasture alone again.

The moral of the story is: Outwit your enemy to save your skin.

9. ThinkSpeakListen

How was the kid able to "outwit" the wolf?

Use Conjunctions to Connect Ideas

	Conjunction	115
"I will go," said Crabb. "My wife, Grete, must come, too," said Crabb.	**but**	"I will go **but** my wife, Grete, must come, too," said Crabb.
The lord bellowed. The first servant came with a dish of delicate fare.	**and**	The lord bellowed **and** the first servant came with a dish of delicate fare.
Now what Crabb meant was that he was the servant who brought the first dish. The servant thought Crabb meant that he was the first thief—which he actually was. He was terrified.	**but** **and**	Now what Crabb meant was that he was the servant who brought the first dish, **but** the servant thought that Crabb meant that he was the first thief—which he actually was—**and** he was terrified.

10. ThinkSpeakListen

Compare and contrast the ways Crabb and the girl from "The Three Spinsters" solve their problems. Make sure to use conjunctions to help you connect your ideas.

The Wolf and the Fox by the Brothers Grimm

1 Wolf and Fox were always together…. Wolf was strong like an ox, while Fox was weak like a reed. So Wolf was the master over Fox.

2 Poor Fox was compelled to do whatever Wolf wished. Now, secretly Fox sought ways that he might get rid of his master once and for all….

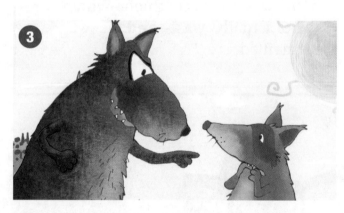

3 Wolf turned to his small friend and said, "I am hungry. Fox, you simply must seize me some food or else I will starve…. And if you don't find me food, I will have to eat you."…

4 *I have to do something about this situation,* said Fox to himself. Then he said aloud, "I know a man who has killed a large pig. The savory, salted meat is in a barrel in the cellar."

11. ThinkSpeakListen

Use adjectives and adverbs to describe Wolf and Fox.

Wolf smiled, and so Fox and Wolf set off for the cellar. They found a small hole in the cellar wall and squeezed through.

In the cellar, there was indeed much meat, and Wolf attacked it right away. Fox liked it too, but Fox also kept running to the hole where they had come in.

Fox wanted to make sure that after eating, his body was still skinny enough to slip through the hole. So Fox just nibbled at the food.

Meanwhile, Wolf kept gobbling and gobbling. Finally, he saw Fox running to the hole. "Why are you running here and there?"

Fox, being crafty, replied, "I must see that no one is coming." Wolf nodded and kept eating. "Don't eat too much," warned Fox.

Wolf ignored this warning.... The farmer heard Fox running about and Wolf slurping, and he raced into the cellar.

When Fox saw the farmer, he bounded into the hole and was gone in a flash. Wolf wanted to follow, but with his full belly he got stuck in the hole.

Needless to say, it was Wolf's last meal. Fox was safely away in the forest, very pleased to finally be rid of his gluttonous master.

12. ThinkSpeakListen

Compare Fox with the brave goose from "The Fox and the Geese." Which character do you think came up with a better solution to his problem?

Use Prepositional Phrases to Add Detail

Wolf turned **to his small friend** and said, "I am hungry."

The savory, salted meat is **in a barrel in the cellar**.

Fox wanted to make sure that after eating, his body was still skinny enough to slip **through the hole**.

Fox was safely away **in the forest**, very pleased to finally be rid of his gluttonous master.

13. ThinkSpeakListen

Describe how Fox was able to get rid of Wolf. Use prepositional phrases to add detail to your description.

Canine Cousins: The Fox and the Wolf

The fox and the wolf are animals often found in fairy tales or folktales. Both are members of the canine family, which also includes dogs.... Like dogs, they have long legs, a large chest, and a long snout. They communicate through barks, growls, and yelps....

Wolves are larger than foxes and have gray, red, or brown fur. They live and hunt in packs of six to ten. Together, they can bring down moose, deer, or other large prey....

Foxes are smaller than wolves, with narrower snouts and bushy tails. The fox is often pictured with red fur, but its fur may be brown, gray, or even yellow.

14. ThinkSpeakListen

Use descriptive words and compound sentences to compare and contrast wolves and foxes.

Building Research Skills

<u>While some people think that stories by the Brothers Grimm teach good values (such as being smart and having courage), other people think that these stories promote bad behavior (such as lying and tricking people).</u> Read and take notes about two other stories by the Brothers Grimm. Look for evidence to help you formulate an opinion based on this question: Are the Brothers Grimm teaching people to be good, or to be bad?

Subject

Research focus

Research goal

Paraphrase to Avoid Plagiarism

Original Text

Gretel cried bitter tears and said to Hansel, "It is over with us!"

"Be quiet, Gretel," said Hansel, "and don't worry. I know what to do."

Synonyms and Restatements

bitter—sharp and resentful

Gretel is crying. She seems emotional: sad, angry, and afraid.

Hansel seems able to take charge. He also seems to care for Gretel.

Paraphrase

Gretel is crying. She seems to be feeling resentful, sad, and afraid. Hansel, however, is able to take charge, and tells Gretel not to worry, because he has a plan.

Essential Question

What is a community?

My Language Objectives

- Use prepositional phrases to add details about place
- Write a compare/contrast essay
- Use prepositional phrases to add details about time
- Identify connections within a text
- Form and use irregular verbs
- Combine prepositional phrases to add detail

My Content Objectives

- Build vocabulary related to community
- Understand what a community is

an urban community

a diverse community

a rural community

Exploring My Community by Lisa Benjamin

As the sun rises, my little city begins to wake.... All around St. Augustine, Florida, restaurant and hotel workers welcome tourists and other visitors.

1 A community is any place that people call home. Mine is on the coast of the Atlantic Ocean. We have beaches and wetland areas. Today is cool for December: 18 degrees Celsius (65 degrees Fahrenheit). (I know, lucky me!)...

Pedro Menéndez de Avilés

I am proud of St. Augustine. It is the oldest city in the United States, founded in 1565 by Pedro Menéndez de Avilés. He was an explorer from Spain.

History is important in my community.... Keeping the old buildings in good shape keeps the past alive and makes sense for business, too.

1. ThinkSpeakListen

Describe the community of St. Augustine, Florida.

Use Prepositional Phrases to Add Details About Place

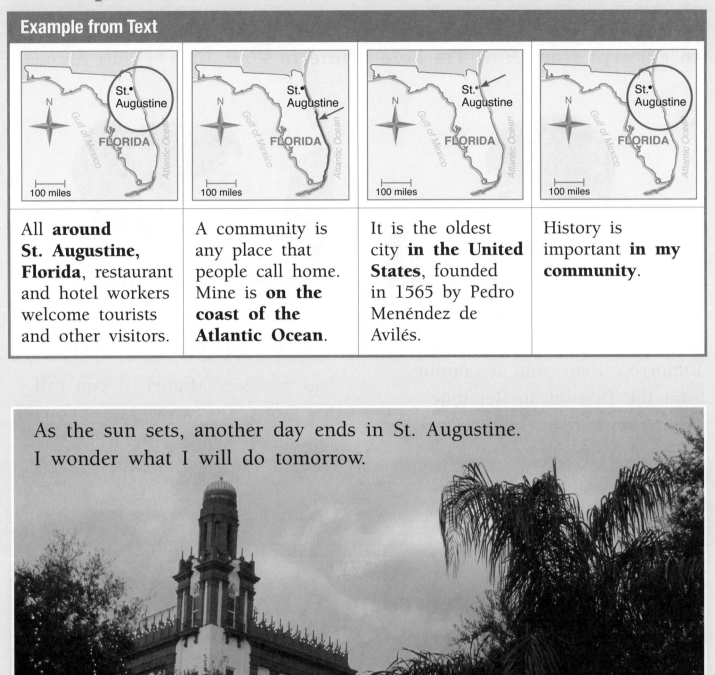

All **around St. Augustine, Florida**, restaurant and hotel workers welcome tourists and other visitors.

A community is any place that people call home. Mine is **on the coast of the Atlantic Ocean**.

It is the oldest city **in the United States**, founded in 1565 by Pedro Menéndez de Avilés.

History is important **in my community**.

As the sun sets, another day ends in St. Augustine. I wonder what I will do tomorrow.

2. ThinkSpeakListen
Use prepositional phrases to describe your own community.

A New Life in Vermont

an excerpt from *How Tía Lola Came to ~~Visit~~ Stay* by Julia Alvarez

"Why can't we just call her *Aunt* Lola?" Miguel asks his mother. Tomorrow their aunt is coming from the Dominican Republic to visit with them in their new home in Vermont....

"Because she doesn't know any English," his mother explains....

"So you see, Miguel, if you call her Aunt, she won't know you're talking to her."...

It is the last day of January.... Miguel and Juanita's parents are getting a divorce, and Mami has been hired to be a counselor in a small college in Vermont....

Mami does not like the idea of Miguel and Juanita being alone without an adult, and that in large part is why she has invited Tía Lola to come for a visit.

126

Why not ask Papi to come up and stay with them instead? Miguel wants to suggest. He doesn't really understand why his parents can't stay married even if they don't get along....

But Miguel doesn't dare suggest this to her. These days, Mami bursts out crying at anything. When they first drove up to the old house with its peeling white paint, Mami's eyes filled with tears.

"It looks haunted," Juanita gasped.

"It looks like a dump," Miguel corrected his little sister. "Even Dracula wouldn't live here."

But then, catching a glimpse of his mother's sad face, he added quickly, "So you don't have to worry about ghosts, Nita!"

His mother smiled through her tears, grateful to him for being a good sport.

3. ThinkSpeakListen

Compare and contrast the ways Miguel and the author of "Exploring My Community" feel about their communities.

The Mission District

Let's take a trip to the Mission District of San Francisco, California!… Today the Mission District draws visitors from around the world.… In the streets, the rich scent of Mexican food fills the air. Restaurants serve traditional tamales and tacos. Bakers and grocers offer tasty Mexican treats.

Special events also draw visitors to the Mission District.… In May, a large carnival draws thousands of people. Carnival-goers enjoy food from street vendors. Musicians, dancers, and actors entertain the crowds.

Yet the Mission District is more than food and festivals. It's also a neighborhood. Workers, business owners, and families make it their home.… Murals and artwork by and about Latinos fill outdoor spaces.… The Mission District is a thriving community and home to people proud of their roots.

4. ThinkSpeakListen

Which community is more like the Mission District: St. Augustine or Vermont? Support your ideas with specific text evidence.

Writing to Sources

"Exploring My Community," "How Tía Lola Came to ~~Visit~~ Stay," and the Unit 1 text "Working Together" all present different pictures of what a community is. Write an essay in which you compare and contrast these different pictures of community.

Sample Essay

The word "community" means different things to different people. The texts "Exploring My Community," "How Tía Lola Came to ~~Visit~~ Stay," and "Working Together" all show the different ways people form communities.

The first paragraph introduces the topic and lets the reader know how you will support your ideas.

For the author of "Exploring My Community," "community" is the place where you live. When she writes about her community of St. Augustine, she focuses on its history, how it is near the ocean, and how it has many beautiful old buildings.

However, in "How Tía Lola Came to ~~Visit~~ Stay," "community" has more to do with the people around you. In this story, the members of Miguel's family come together to help each other during a difficult time. Tía Lola agrees to visit to make sure the children are not left alone. Miguel tries to cheer his mother up when she is sad. Since they are in a strange new place, the family members make their own little "community."

The body paragraphs develop the topic with details and evidence from your sources.

"Working Together" also shows how community is about people helping one another. When a storm threatens to flood Fargo, North Dakota, its citizens work hard to keep the town's people and buildings safe. By working together to build walls of sandbags, they are able to keep Fargo from flooding.

"Exploring My Community," "How Tía Lola Came to ~~Visit~~ Stay," and "Working Together" all show the different ways people think about communities. No matter where you live, "community" is all about making the most of your surroundings, and cooperating with the people around you.

The last paragraph provides a concluding statement.

All Kinds of Communities by Lisa Benjamin

Farmersville, a Rural Community
by Mason Streeter

1

My town, Farmersville, is in a rural area of northern Texas.... Dallas is only thirty-five miles away. We can drive there in half an hour....

2

Farmers have called this place home since 1849.... Those first settlers planted cotton, which became a big part of the area's economy....

3

Then one farmer planted onions, and that turned into a bumper crop!... Onions became so big that the community started an "Onion Festival" in 1935....

4

Today, many people in Farmersville still work in farming.... People come from all over—even big city Dallas—to buy my community's fresh-grown food.

5. ThinkSpeakListen
Why is farming so important to the community of Farmersville?

St. Louis, a River Community
by Keisha Paul

5

The Mississippi River cuts through the middle of my city. With such easy access to water, it's no wonder many people here enjoy boating and fishing.

6

The Mississippi has affected the community in other ways, too.... The river was...the starting point for people moving west in the 1800s. That's how St. Louis got the nickname "Gateway to the West."...

7

The Mississippi River also helped create businesses. People built factories along the riverbanks. Also, ships could travel in and out of the city to deliver goods....

8

Tourism is another important business. Visitors come from all over the world to see the mighty Mississippi and other sights, like the famous Gateway Arch....

Los Angeles, a Diverse Community
by Gabriel Garcia

9

Los Angeles is one of the biggest cities in the country. More than four million people live in the city....

10

The population of Los Angeles (L.A.) is not only big. It is also diverse!... More than 200 languages are spoken in L.A.

11

Native Americans were the first people to make this area their home. Spanish settlers came in the 1700s.... Since then, many other groups have moved here....

12

Today, Latinos make up the biggest group.... My family came from Mexico long ago.... Immigrants have brought their culture to this community and helped make it a fun place.

6. ThinkSpeakListen
Compare and contrast the communities of Farmersville, St. Louis, and Los Angeles. Which community would you want to live in? Why?

Use Prepositional Phrases to Add Details About Time

Farmers have called this place home **since 1849**.	1800 1849 1900 2000
Onions became so big that the community started an "Onion Festival" **in 1935**.	TEXAS 10/15 SWEET ONION $4.⁰⁰/bunch 1800 1900 1935 2000
The river was...the starting point for people moving west **in the 1800s**.	1800 1900 2000
Spanish settlers came **in the 1700s**. **Since then**, many other groups have moved here.	1700 1800 1900 2000

7. ThinkSpeakListen

Use prepositional phrases to describe the history of one of the communities described in "All Kinds of Communities."

133

The Levi Coffin House

On a street in what is now Fountain City, Indiana, there is a redbrick house.... The house is the Levi Coffin House. It was a main stop along the Underground Railroad.

The Underground Railroad was a network that helped enslaved people escape to freedom in the 1800s.... Levi Coffin was an important part of this network.... He opposed slavery, so he'd take many risks for his beliefs.

In 1839, Coffin and his wife moved to the redbrick house.... It had eight rooms, many with two exits.... Coffin's neighbors would sew new clothes for the escapees to wear. The escapees ate and slept in safety.... It is said that everyone who hid in Levi Coffin's house made it to freedom. Today the Levi Coffin House is a National Historic Landmark.

Levi Coffin

8. ThinkSpeakListen

Why do you think the Levi Coffin House was such a perfect house for people on the Underground Railroad to use?

Identify Connections Within a Text

Farmers have called this place home since 1849. The area's fertile, black soil was perfect for growing crops.	Those first settlers planted cotton, which became a big part of the area's economy.
The river was…the starting point for people moving west in the 1800s.	That's how St. Louis got the nickname "Gateway to the West."
Spanish settlers came in the 1700s.	Since then, many other groups have moved here.
The Underground Railroad was a network that helped enslaved people.	Levi Coffin was an important part of this network.

9. ThinkSpeakListen

Describe a day in your community. Use words such as *this*, *that*, and *those* to condense your ideas.

Sarah and the Chickens

an excerpt from *Sarah, Plain and Tall*

by Patricia MacLachlan

It is the late 1800s in the newly developed farmland of the west. Sarah, a young woman from Maine, answers an ad to become a wife for Jacob, a widower. Caleb and Anna, Jacob's children, fall in love with Sarah. Life on the prairie is different and demanding, and Sarah misses the sea. Will she stay longer than the one month to which she has agreed?

Our neighbors, Matthew and Maggie, came to help Papa plow up a new field for corn. Sarah stood with us on the porch, watching their wagon wind up the road, two horses pulling it and one tied in back....

Matthew and Maggie came with their two children and a sackful of chickens. Maggie emptied the sack into the yard and three red banty chickens clucked and scattered....

10. ThinkSpeakListen

Which community from "All Kinds of Communities" is most like the one described in this story? Cite specific text evidence to support your answer.

Sarah loved the chickens. She clucked back to them and fed them grain. They followed her, shuffling and scratching primly in the dirt. I knew they would not be for eating....

"I nearly forgot," said Maggie on the porch. "I have something more for you."...

"Plants," she said to Sarah. "For your garden."

"My garden?" Sarah bent down to touch the plants.

"Zinnias and marigolds and wild feverfew," said Maggie. "You must have a garden. Wherever you are."...

We planted the flowers by the porch, turning over the soil and patting it around them, and watering.... In the fields, the horses pulled the plow up and down under the hot summer sun....

"Soon you can drive your wagon over to my house and I will give you more…."

Sarah frowned. "I have never driven a wagon."

"I can teach you," said Maggie….

Way off in the sky, clouds gathered. Matthew and Papa and Caleb came in from the fields, their work done. We all ate in the shade.

"We are glad you are here," said Matthew to Sarah. "A new friend. Maggie misses her friends sometimes."

Sarah nodded. "There is always something to miss, no matter where you are," she said, smiling at Maggie.

11. ThinkSpeakListen

Do you think Sarah will stay longer than the one month to which she has agreed? Cite specific text evidence to support your answer.

Form and Use Irregular Verbs

Example from "Sarah and the Chickens"	Present Tense	Past Tense
Sarah **stood** with us on the porch, watching their wagon wind up the road, two horses pulling it and one tied in back.	stand	stood
She clucked back to them and **fed** them grain.	feed	fed
"I nearly **forgot**," said Maggie on the porch.	forget	forgot
Sarah **bent** down to touch the plants.	bend	bent
We all **ate** in the shade.	eat	ate

12. ThinkSpeakListen
Use the past tense of these irregular verbs to describe a day in your community.

Wind and Wildflowers

The tall grass is gently waving in the wind. I can see colorful wildflowers peeking out between the stalks. Spring is beautiful on the prairie. It almost makes me forget about the awful winter that just passed.

It was my first winter on the prairie. Father and Uncle Paul had come out here before Mother and me. They built a sod house for us to live in.... They stacked the sod bricks to form walls. Even the roof of the house was made from sod. When Mother and I arrived, the small "soddy" house was ready for us. And when cold weather came, it was surprisingly warm inside....

The ground is finally thawing now, and summer will soon be here.... But hot weather also brings storms, and maybe even a tornado or two.... It is not easy to live here. Yet, when I pause to gaze out at the prairie at dawn, I know this place has captured my heart.

13. ThinkSpeakListen

Based on your reading, explain what made life so hard for settlers on the prairie.

140

Combine Prepositional Phrases to Add Detail

Sarah stood…	
Sarah stood **with us**.	
Sarah stood with us **on the porch**.	
…the horses pulled the plow…	
In the fields, the horses pulled the plow.	
In the fields, the horses pulled the plow **up and down under the hot summer sun**.	

14. ThinkSpeakListen

Combine prepositional phrases to create a more detailed description of your community.

Essential Question

How can we predict the unknown?

thunderstorm

My Language Objectives

- Understand nonliteral language: metaphor
- Use concrete and abstract nouns
- Use the language of sequence
- Use the language of comparison
- Research and write a narrative essay

My Content Objectives

- Build vocabulary related to weather and climate
- Understand how patterns can be observed and recorded to predict the unknown

satellite view of hurricane

flash flooding

Fairweather Clouds

by Carmen Corriols

1   Here,
after the thaw
these plains, a green sea,
encircle me

5   Now I tilt my head back,
splay[1] my hands, pressing
into the fresh waves of prairie.

Above, the sky,
the blue field,
10   is thick with piles of
cumulus[2] cotton,
ripe for picking,
stuffing and quilting,
heaping and billowing[3] about,
15   but still
bright and clean
in the sun.

Later, when they grow gray
and nimbus,[4]
20   the rain will come.

1 splay—to spread out
2 cumulus—white, puffy cloud with a flat base that
   indicates little or no precipitation

3 billowing—filling up and swelling outward
4 nimbus—large gray rain cloud

1. ThinkSpeakListen

Summarize the main idea of this poem, pointing to text evidence to back up your idea.

Understand Nonliteral Language: Metaphor

these plains, a green sea

pressing into the fresh
waves of prairie. (grassy hills)

the sky, the blue field

piles of
cumulus cotton   (clouds)

2. ThinkSpeakListen

Explain how the reference to cotton helps this poem describe the clouds over the prairie.

Earth's Weather and Climate by Laura McDonald

Weather describes the atmosphere's conditions in a certain place at a given moment in time....

Climate describes the average weather patterns of that place over long periods of time. Climate describes the average weather of the seasons....

How do scientists track these weather patterns? Scientists measure...temperature, which is how hot or cold a place is. They measure the amount of precipitation that falls as rain, snow, or sleet from the sky....

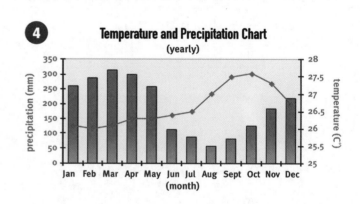

Temperature and Precipitation Chart
(yearly)

Scientists use different tools to measure these factors.... Then they use this data to figure out the weather patterns of a region. Using this information, they can define the climate type.

146

5

Some climates are hot and rainy.... regions closer to the equator receive more direct sunlight. As a result, they tend to be warmer. Places closer to water have more moisture.... As a result, they tend to get more rainfall.

6

Regions far from the equator tend to be cold. Places far from water tend to be dry....

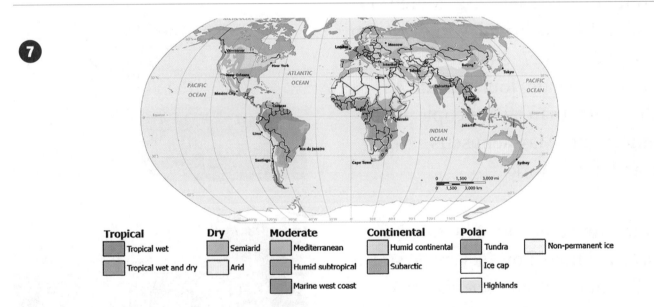

7

Tropical	Dry	Moderate	Continental	Polar	
Tropical wet	Semiarid	Mediterranean	Humid continental	Tundra	Non-permanent ice
Tropical wet and dry	Arid	Humid subtropical	Subarctic	Ice cap	
		Marine west coast		Highlands	

As a result, Earth has several different climate zones: tropical, dry, moderate, continental, and polar. Each climate has its own characteristics.

Each climate also supports its own diverse forms of plant and animal life. Understanding a region's climate helps people predict what typical weather will be like throughout the year.

3. ThinkSpeakListen

Use a metaphor to describe one of the pictures in this text.

Blizzard Alert!

Blizzards are severe winter storms. They can cover whole towns in a blanket of white snow. Blizzards have high winds, below-freezing temperatures, and blinding snowfall. Some can last several days. Depending on its size and duration, a blizzard can even affect several states.

One of the worst cases…was the Great Blizzard of 1888. On March 11 and March 12,…a brutal winter storm dumped 100 to 127 cm (40 to 50 inches) of snow on four states. As a result, more than 400 people died in Connecticut, Massachusetts, New Jersey, and New York.…

At that time, people did not have any way to know how severe a storm would be. Since then, science has come a long way. Today we can use computers and satellite images to predict where a storm will go.…Planning for proper snow and ice removal in these emergencies can save lives.

4. ThinkSpeakListen

State your opinion on the following question: How can weather predictions save lives?

Use <u>Concrete</u> and <u>Abstract</u> Nouns

Example from Text	Noun	Type of Noun
They can cover whole towns in a <u>blanket</u> of white snow.	blanket	concrete
A blizzard can even affect several <u>states</u>.	states	concrete
Depending on its <u>size</u> and <u>duration</u>, a blizzard…	size/duration	abstract
Planning for proper snow and ice <u>removal</u> in these emergencies can save lives.	removal	abstract

5. ThinkSpeakListen

Describe weather using concrete and abstract nouns.

Water Sky

by Jean Craighead George

A boy in a bright blue ski jacket and Maine hunting boots stood on a snowy runway.... He was not amused.... Yesterday he had left Boston.... Now he was about to run back to the friendly jet that had carried him across Alaska to this barren Arctic outpost.

Suddenly, a cloud of frozen fog swirled over him. He could not see the plane, or the sky, or the flat snowscape that rolled endlessly out beyond the airport. Wrapped in an Arctic whiteout, he could have been upside down or sidewise for all he could tell....

In a few moments he was standing in the sunshine again, and the terror of the tundra blew off.

He turned and ran to the airport terminal, his face happy with purpose. He was going to do what he had come to Barrow, Alaska, to do....

6. ThinkSpeakListen

Summarize what has happened so far in this story. Be sure to identify the characters involved, the time when the story takes place, and the setting.

"You will know me by my blue-rimmed sunglasses," Vincent Ologak had said. The boy glanced from face to face. There was no one with blue-rimmed sunglasses.

"You Lincoln Noah Stonewright?" The boy spun around, and his eyes met those of another boy.

"Yes, yes, I am."

"I am Kusiq....

...I'm glad you're here." His exceptionally dark eyes were slanted upward as if he were perpetually smiling. His cheeks were broad and high, like those of the Eskimos in the painting that hung above the fireplace in Lincoln's home....

The painting depicted his great-great-grandfather's whaling ship frozen into the Arctic ice for the winter. Kids like Kusiq were playing baseball on the ice with the adult Eskimos and the Yankee whalers.... Lincoln managed to smile at Kusiq.

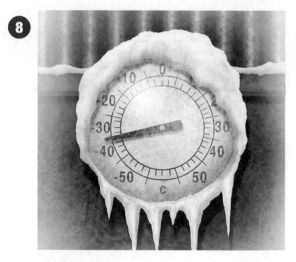

"Vincent Ologak is sorry he cannot meet you," Kusiq said. "He is not well." Lincoln breathed deeply to quell the panic that was rising in him.... "He sent me to get you.... I will take you home first. You can leave your bags there." Lincoln nodded.... He followed Kusiq out of the terminal....

He looked out on the village of Barrow.... Then he saw two four-wheel-drive vehicles that had been left running so they would not freeze up.... And then he saw why. The large thermometer on the side of the terminal registered thirty-five below zero....

His dad was right. This was going to be a wonderful adventure. "Hop on," Kusiq said. "I'll give you a tour."... Lincoln swung onto the seat behind Kusiq.... The machine shot forward.... "I am not on my planet," Lincoln said to himself. "Barrow is not just 'different,' as Dad says; it is otherworldly."

7. ThinkSpeakListen
Recount one problem that occurs in this story, and how the problem is solved.

Use the Language of Sequence

Example from Text	Word or Phrase That Indicates Sequence
"He sent me to get you.... I will take you home **first**. You can leave your bags there."	**first**
Yesterday he had left Boston.... **Now** he was about to run back to the friendly jet that had carried him across Alaska to this barren Arctic outpost.	**Yesterday/Now**
Suddenly, a cloud of frozen fog swirled over him.	**Suddenly**
He looked out on the village of Barrow.... **Then** he saw two four-wheel-drive vehicles that had been left running so they would not freeze up.... And **then** he saw why.	**Then**

8. ThinkSpeakListen

Recount the events of your day so far, using at least two of the sequence indicators listed above.

How Indian Summer Began

Long ago there was a generous...man named Notkikad. He was a good farmer. One year...there was a late frost and his garden died. He planted it again and then there came a drought....

...Without...corn, squash, and beans, they would not survive.... The leaves were falling...the freezing winds blew.

One night, he spoke to the Master of Life. "I have...never asked for help, but... What can I do?"... In his dream, the Master came to him. "I am giving you these special seeds," the Master said. "I am also giving you a time in which to plant them."

When Notkikad awoke, he found the seeds. He went outside and though the leaves were still falling, the weather was now as warm as summer. He and his family planted all the seeds. The next morning,... Green shoots rose out of the soil.... The special seeds given to him grew rapidly in only a handful of days of the Indian summer.

9. ThinkSpeakListen
Describe the personality traits that you can identify in Notkikad.

Research and Writing

Imagine that you are preparing for a severe weather event. Conduct research to find out how you will prepare and what you will experience when this weather arrives. Write a fictional firsthand account of the storm.

Topic for research/writing

Research focus

Purpose for writing

Plan a Narrative

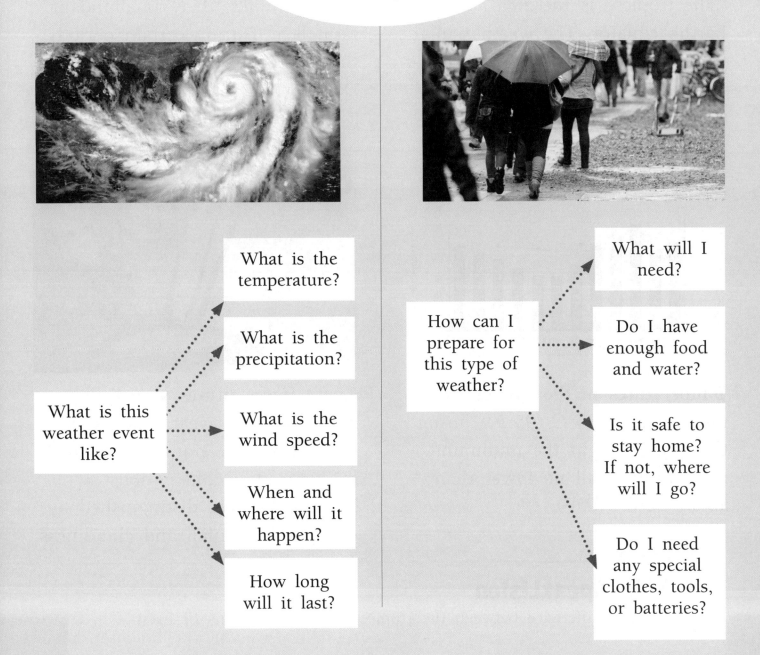

What severe weather event will I plan for?

What is this weather event like?

- What is the temperature?
- What is the precipitation?
- What is the wind speed?
- When and where will it happen?
- How long will it last?

How can I prepare for this type of weather?

- What will I need?
- Do I have enough food and water?
- Is it safe to stay home? If not, where will I go?
- Do I need any special clothes, tools, or batteries?

The Tropical Rain Belt

adapted from National Oceanic and Atmospheric Administration (NOAA.gov)

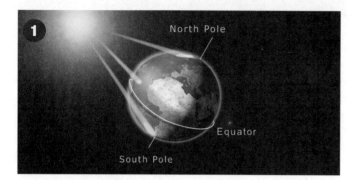

"The tropics" is the area along Earth's equator. The weather in the tropics is mostly hot and humid. …due to the tropics receiving more energy from the sun….

In the tropics, there is abundant rainfall…. During certain periods, thunderstorms can occur every day. Despite this, the tropics still receive a great deal of sunshine….

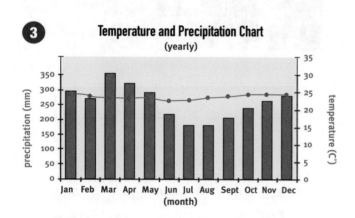

Temperatures in the tropics rarely exceed 35°C (95°F) during the day. At night the minimum temperatures fall no lower than about 22°C (72°F).

These temperatures vary little throughout the year. Therefore, the seasons are not distinguished by warm and cold periods. Instead they are distinguished by changes in rainfall and cloudiness.

10. ThinkSpeakListen

Explain one difference between the tropics and other regions of Earth.

The "tropical rain belt" appears as a band of clouds. These clouds encircle the globe near the equator. They cause frequent showers and occasional thunderstorms....

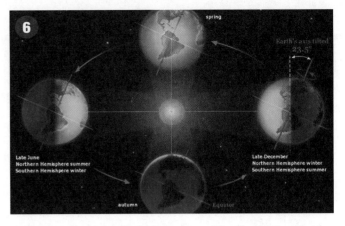

Scientists call this "rain belt" the Intertropical Convergence Zone (ITCZ) (pronounced "itch"). The ITCZ follows the sun.... It moves north in the northern summer and south in the northern winter. The ITCZ causes the wet and dry seasons in the tropics.

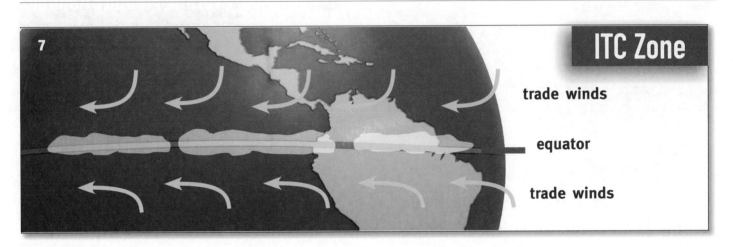

ITC Zone

trade winds

equator

trade winds

The ITCZ is caused by the trade winds. The trade winds meet, or converge, at the equator. In the Northern Hemisphere the trade winds move in a southwest direction.

In the Southern Hemisphere they move in a northwest direction. The point at which the trade winds converge forces the air up into the atmosphere. This forms the ITCZ.

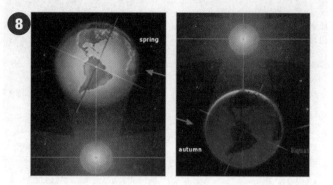

In the tropics, storms tend to be short.... But they can produce intense rainfall.... Greatest rainfall occurs when the sun is directly over the equator.... in March and September. As a result, there are two wet and two dry seasons.

Farther away from the equator, the two rainy seasons merge into one. Here the climate becomes more monsoonal, with one wet season and one dry season....

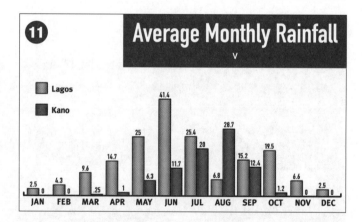

One prime example of the effects of the ITCZ can be witnessed in Nigeria. Because of its location just north of the equator, Nigeria's climate has hot and wet conditions.

These are due to the movement of the ITCZ north and south of the equator. This can be seen in the monthly rainfall for two cities, Kano and Lagos, separated by 800 km (500 miles).

11. ThinkSpeakListen

Explain how a region's distance from the equator affects its climate. How does this factor impact the climate where you live?

Use the Language of Comparison

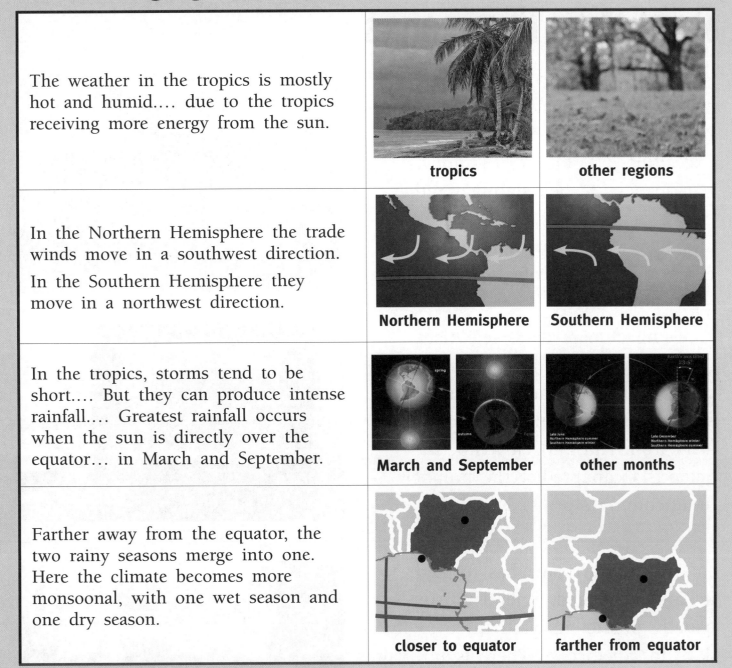

The weather in the tropics is mostly hot and humid.... due to the tropics receiving more energy from the sun.

tropics **other regions**

In the Northern Hemisphere the trade winds move in a southwest direction.
In the Southern Hemisphere they move in a northwest direction.

Northern Hemisphere **Southern Hemisphere**

In the tropics, storms tend to be short.... But they can produce intense rainfall.... Greatest rainfall occurs when the sun is directly over the equator... in March and September.

March and September **other months**

Farther away from the equator, the two rainy seasons merge into one. Here the climate becomes more monsoonal, with one wet season and one dry season.

closer to equator **farther from equator**

12. ThinkSpeakListen
Compare two things in the classroom, using the terms identified in these examples.

159

Predicting Hurricanes

A hurricane is a type of severe tropical cyclone. It has thunderstorms and winds exceeding 119 kmph (74 mph). Hurricanes are devastating weather events. They can destroy homes and lives. They can flood whole cities and erode crops.

Using climate data, scientists can predict when hurricanes are most likely to occur. Hurricane season in the Northern Hemisphere lasts from April to November. Scientists can predict the number of upcoming storms....

Once a hurricane has formed, it can be tracked. Scientists can usually predict its path three to five days in advance.... There is no way to know what will be destroyed. But knowing when and where it will hit can help people stay out of harm's way.

13. ThinkSpeakListen

Why is climate data collection important? Is this information helpful or unhelpful? Explain your thoughts.

Research and Writing

Topic for research/writing

Research focus

Purpose for writing

Sample Essay

Last October, I learned an important lesson. A large hurricane was spotted off the coast of Florida. Within a few days, meteorologists predicted it would make landfall not far from my hometown. I was scared and nervous, but once we began preparing for the storm, I became less fearful. Instead, I was filled with a calm sense of purpose.

The introduction presents the main character, setting, and situation.

We first heard the news reports during breakfast, three days before the storm. It was a typical sunny Monday. But the weather reporter on our local news channel said that a category 4 hurricane was gathering energy over the Gulf and heading our way. We began thinking about how to prepare our home. My mom and I made a list.

Tuesday, we made sure we had enough water and canned food. We also packed small bags with light rain gear in case we needed to evacuate. Since we might lose electricity we charged all of our batteries and checked our flashlights. By Wednesday, the sky had grown much cloudier and windier than the day before. We boarded up the windows. On Thursday, the storm hit. The howling winds lasted almost all day long, but the worst of the wind and rain hit at low tide, so the flooding was not too terrible.

The body paragraphs use description to develop experiences and events. They also show the responses of characters to situations.

We were lucky we did not have to leave our home. We were able to provide safe shelter to friends and family who live closer to the coastline and who did have to evacuate. I was glad when the storm was finally over. Now I know the most important thing to remember is to stay calm and be prepared!

The conclusion wraps up the narrative.

What do our economic choices tell us about ourselves?

a farmers' market in the United States

My Language Objectives

- Use concrete and abstract nouns
- Use pronouns to identify point of view
- Use the language of time and sequence
- Use subordinating conjunctions to form complex sentences
- Research and write an informative essay

My Content Objectives

- Build vocabulary related to economics and industry
- Understand the types of economic choices that people make

a grocery store

a farmers' market in Peru

163

Making Choices

1 Ben Franklin's "Two Cents"

Benjamin Franklin was one of the Founders of the United States.... Between 1732 and 1758, he published an annual, or yearly, book. Poor Richard's Almanack included stories, useful information about the weather, and valuable household tips. It also included many proverbs, or timeless sayings, about work and money.

Benjamin Franklin

Waste neither time nor money, but make the best use of both.

If a man empties his purse into his head, no one can take it away from him.

The way to wealth depends on just two words: frugality and industry.

Early to bed, early to rise, makes a man healthy, wealthy, and wise.

A penny saved is a penny earned.

1. ThinkSpeakListen

Choose one of Ben Franklin's proverbs and explain in your own words what it means.

Use <u>Concrete</u> and <u>Abstract</u> Nouns

Example from "Ben Franklin's 'Two Cents'"	Noun	Type of Noun
<u>Benjamin Franklin</u> was one of the Founders of the United States.	Benjamin Franklin	concrete
Between 1732 and 1758, he published an annual, or yearly, <u>book</u>.	book	concrete
A <u>penny</u> saved is a <u>penny</u> earned.	penny	concrete
The way to wealth depends on just two words: <u>frugality</u> and <u>industry</u>.	frugality	abstract
	industry	abstract

2. ThinkSpeakListen

Explain the difference between concrete and abstract nouns. Then choose other nouns from the text and identify them as concrete or abstract.

Let It Grow:
The Booming Business of Farmers' Markets

by Lisa Benjamin

Farmers' markets sell fruit, vegetables, and other goods. The goods are local and fresh.

One local business that keeps growing today is the farmers' market. In the last ten years, the number of towns and cities that have farmers' markets has doubled. Today the United States Department of Agriculture (USDA) lists more than 8,000 farmers' markets. And that number keeps growing. Why have these markets become such a hit? Consumer choice!

One choice is to eat more healthfully. Studies show we need to eat fresh greens, fruits, and vegetables. Fresh produce is a healthful part of our diet....

Grocery stores report that fresh produce sales have tripled since the 1990s. Farmers' markets are also meeting this demand....

There is another reason for this success. People are not just making healthful choices for their bodies. They are also trying to make good choices for their communities. For example, they buy local food. This is a good way to support their local farmers.

Food writer Michael Pollan reports: "…By shopping at a farmers' market, you support local agriculture, which has a great many benefits.

"You keep farmers in your community. You keep land from being sprawled with houses and shopping centers. You also have the experience of shopping in a farmers' market!"

3. ThinkSpeakListen

Do you think that shopping in farmers' markets is a good idea? Why or why not?

The Milkmaid

Once there was a girl who milked cows on her mother's small farm. Every morning…the girl would balance a pail of milk on her head. Then she'd walk to market…

One day on the way to market, the girl began to daydream. *After I get money for the milk, I will buy some young chickens,* she thought. *They will begin laying eggs, and I'll sell the eggs…*

My business will become quite profitable. Then I'll buy beautiful clothes… Everyone will be envious of me….

The delightful daydream seemed so real the girl actually gave her head a playful toss. With that, the pail tumbled off her head…The tearful girl returned home that day without selling a drop of milk.

"Silly child," her mother said. "You'll be penniless if you only daydream about what you want."

4. ThinkSpeakListen
Describe the milkmaid's personality.

Use Pronouns to Identify Point of View

Once there was a girl who milked cows on **her** mother's small farm. Every morning…the girl would balance a pail of milk on **her** head. Then **she**'d walk to market.

*My business will become quite profitable. Then I'll buy beautiful clothes…Everyone will be envious of **me**.*

First Person Pronouns

	Subject	Object	Possessive
Singular	I	me	my
Plural	we	us	our

Third Person Pronouns

	Subject	Object	Possessive
Singular	he	him	his
	she	her	her
	it	it	its
Plural	they	them	their

5. ThinkSpeakListen

Explain what you think the lesson of "The Milkmaid" is. Use first person and third person pronouns in your discussion.

Lazy Harry by the Brothers Grimm

Long ago, there lived a boy named Harry. This boy was lazy and disliked working. Though all he did for work was to look after his goat, Harry still found this simple task to be exhausting....

Suddenly, a good idea, clear as day, came upon him.... He would marry his neighbor Trina, who also had a goat. She could take her goat with Harry's, and then Harry would not have to work....

Trina became Harry's wife. She led out both the goats. Harry had a good time of it and no work....

But, wouldn't you know it, Trina was lazy, too! She did not like to watch the goats any more than Harry did....

Finally, an idea came to her. "Dear Harry," she said, "...We should trade our two goats, whose bleating wakes us up too early, to our neighbor. He will give us a beehive.... We will not have to do any work. Bees do not require work.... We can collect honey while barely lifting a finger."...

Harry and Trina were happy with the trade... That autumn, Harry filled a jar with honey.

The couple placed the jar on a board fixed to the wall of their bedroom.... Trina brought in a stout hazel-stick. She put the stick beside her bed so she could easily reach it without getting up if she needed to drive away any unwanted guests....

6. ThinkSpeakListen
Summarize what has happened so far in this story.

One afternoon when Harry was still lying amongst the feathers in broad daylight, he said to his wife, "…You are always tasting the honey. It will be better for us to exchange it for a goose with a young gosling, before you gobble it all up."…

"But," answered Trina, "not before we have a child to take care of them!"…

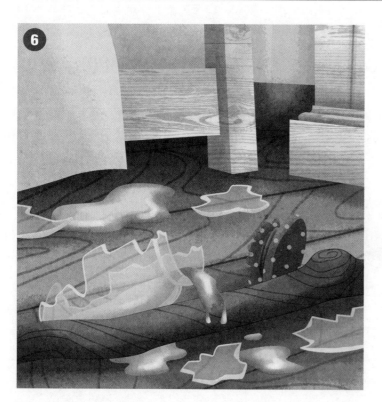

"Oh," replied Trina, "our child shall fare badly if he does not do what I say!" Trina shook the stick and…accidentally hit the honey jar. The jar hit the wall, broke into pieces, and the delicious honey poured out onto the floor.

7. ThinkSpeakListen

What do you think that Harry and Trina will do now?

Use the Language of Time and Sequence

Example from Text	Word or Phrase That Indicates Time
Long ago, there lived a boy named Harry.	Long ago
One afternoon when Harry was still lying amongst the feathers in broad daylight, he said to his wife…	One afternoon

Example from Text	Word or Phrase That Indicates Time or Sequence
She could take her goat with Harry's, and **then** Harry would not have to work.	then
Finally, an idea came to her.	Finally
"But," answered Trina, "not **before** we have a child to take care of them!"	before

8. ThinkSpeakListen

Recount the events of your day so far, using at least two of the sequence indicators listed above.

Two Foolish Brothers

Fred and Finn decided to make some money selling their goods at a village market....

The brothers set up booths across from each other. Business was slow, and Fred hadn't eaten. He found a quarter in his pocket and went to Finn's booth to buy a peach....

Soon, Finn grew hungry. So he went to Fred's booth and bought an unsalted pretzel. He gave his brother the quarter he had earned....

Back and forth they went, until all the peaches and all the pretzels had disappeared....

When the brothers saw they had only a quarter between them, they grumbled in displeasure....

The unhappy brothers disassembled their booths and walked home.

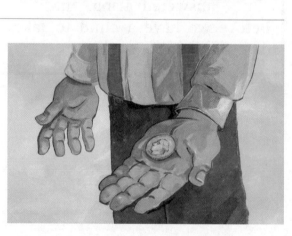

9. ThinkSpeakListen

Locate terms in this story that indicate time or sequence. Identify whether each is a time term or a sequence term.

Research and Writing

Think of a product that you and your family use every day, and research how that product is produced and used. Present your findings in an informative essay.

Topic for research/writing

Research focus

Purpose for writing

Organize Research

My Topic:

How are automobiles produced and used?

Information Learned from My Research

- Assembly-line mass production
- Shared parts
- Shipping goods
- Commuting to work
- Locations: U.S.A., Japan, Europe
- Human labor
- Leisure travel
- Robot assembly
- Auto racing

How are automobiles produced?

- Assembly-line mass production
- Shared parts
- Locations: U.S.A., Japan, Europe
- Human labor
- Robot assembly

How are automobiles used?

- Shipping goods
- Commuting to work
- Leisure travel
- Auto racing

From Fruit to Jam:
A Tasty List of Choices by Alan Wood

Jam is a very popular product around the world. At the breakfast table, it sweetens slices of toast. In the lunchroom, it is the perfect companion to peanut butter on a sandwich....

Like jelly, jam is a preserve made from fruit. There are dozens of different flavors. One of the most popular is orange marmalade....

The first step to making orange marmalade is to produce the fruit. Farmers grow the oranges on trees in orchards....

When the oranges are ready, workers pick them. Then the oranges are sent to factories known as food-processing plants. Now the work of jam-making can really begin....

The entire process takes several steps.

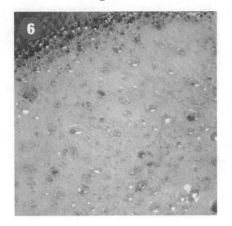

The oranges are crushed.

The precrushed oranges are boiled with sugar and other ingredients.

The crushed fruit mixture is then cooled....

Companies...must choose which kind of sugar to use. Some use white sugar, while others use raw sugar.

White sugar is often less costly and tastes better, but it is not as healthful as raw sugar. Companies can also choose to add other ingredients, like ginger, to change the flavor of the marmalade.

10. ThinkSpeakListen

Recount the steps involved in making orange marmalade.

After the orange marmalade has been produced, it must be packaged. Most companies package jam in glass jars. This keeps it fresh.

They also print labels for the jars. The front label often has an eye-catching image to attract customers in stores....

After the marmalade has been packaged, it is ready to be shipped to stores for restocking the shelves. Trains and trucks carry the prepackaged product to supermarkets all over the country.

Farmers can also sell their own jam at a farmers' market. Now it is up to consumers to make their choices.

11. ThinkSpeakListen

Explain what types of choices consumers make when buying jam.

Use Subordinating Conjunctions to Form Complex Sentences

	Subordinating Conjunction	
The oranges are ready. Workers pick them.	**When**	**When** the oranges are ready, workers pick them.
The orange marmalade has been produced. It must be packaged.	**After**	**After** the orange marmalade has been produced, it must be packaged.
The marmalade has been packaged. It is ready to be shipped to stores for restocking the shelves.	**After**	**After** the marmalade has been packaged, it is ready to be shipped to stores for restocking the shelves.

12. ThinkSpeakListen
Explain what subordinating conjunctions do and why a writer might use them.

Where Do You Get Your Produce?

Today you can get fresh produce right from the farm. This benefits both you and the farmers in your area.

In some places, families can join a buying club that lets them preorder a weekly box of produce. Clubs like this prearrange to buy from local farmers....

People who live in cities can join a food co-op.... In return for investing in the co-op, members can buy food at a lower cost. Most co-ops offer local fruits and vegetables. They restock their produce section often.

Farmers often open their farms to anyone who wants to pick fresh produce. Picking fresh produce is a fun activity for all family members...

Is it time to reconsider where you get your produce? Look around your community. You're sure to find some interesting choices!

13. ThinkSpeakListen

Explain in your own words some of the ways in which consumers can get fresh produce from local farms.

Research and Writing

Think of a product that you and your family use every day, and research how that product is produced and used. Present your findings in an informative essay.

Topic for research/writing

Research focus

Purpose for writing

Sample Essay

There are more automobiles in the world today than ever before. They are built for a wide variety of uses, including personal transportation, competition, and shipping. As production techniques have improved, automobiles have been used for more and more activities, and have been driven by an increasing number of people.

Automobiles are built on assembly lines in factories all over the world. This production method uses a conveyor belt that moves each automobile from one worker to another. Each worker builds one part of the vehicle, which then moves further down the assembly line, where the next worker constructs a different part of it. In some cases, a robot, such as a mechanical arm, does a part of the job instead of a human worker.

Once automobiles are produced, they are used in many different ways. People drive personal vehicles (such as passenger cars) to school, to work, or on vacation. Race cars are used in competitions that excite crowds all over the world. Also, large trucks, some with as many as 18 wheels, deliver goods to stores, where the products can be sold to customers.

As we move into the future, automobiles are improving in comfort and technology. Passenger cars have advanced temperature controls, and their stereos are better than ever. There are also an increasing number of hybrid automobiles, which run on both gas and electricity; these cars are better for the environment than standard vehicles. Thus, as more and more automobiles are built and driven, they are becoming ever more useful to the people who rely on them.

The introduction presents the essay's main topic.

The body of the essay develops the topic with facts and details.

The final paragraph provides a concluding idea.

How does understanding science help us achieve our goals?

All objects have invisible forces acting upon them at all times.

My Language Objectives

- Use prepositional phrases to add detail
- Understand the language of cause and effect
- Understand the language of sequence
- Distinguish sequential text from procedural text
- Research and write an opinion essay

My Content Objectives

- Build vocabulary related to forces and motion
- Describe how we use physical science to meet goals

When the forces are unbalanced, an object will move.

When the forces are balanced, an object will not move.

Poems of Movement
Excerpts from poems by Robert Louis Stevenson

The Swing

How do you like to go up in a
swing,
Up in the air so blue?…

Till I look down on the garden
    green,
Down on the roof so brown—
Up in the air I go flying again,
Up in the air and down!

The Wind

I saw you toss the kites on high
And blow the birds about the sky;…

I saw the different things you did,

But always you yourself you hid.

I felt you push, I heard you call,

I could not see your self at all—

    O wind, a-blowing all day long,

    O wind that sings so loud a song!

1. ThinkSpeakListen
What do you think the author means when he writes "I saw the different things you did, / But always you yourself you hid"?

Use Prepositional Phrases to Add Detail

do you like to swing?

do you like to go up in a swing?

How do you like to go up in a swing?

How do you like to go up in a swing,
Up in the air so blue?

I saw

I saw you toss the kites

I saw you toss the kites on high

I saw you toss the kites on high
And blow the birds about the sky

I go

Up in the air I go

Up in the air I go flying again,
Up in the air and down!

2. ThinkSpeakListen
Use prepositional phrases to describe your movement.

What Makes Things Move?

by Kathy Furgang

Motion, or movement, is any change in the position of an object. What causes movement? Forces cause movement.

All objects on Earth have forces acting on them at all times. A force can be a push or a pull....

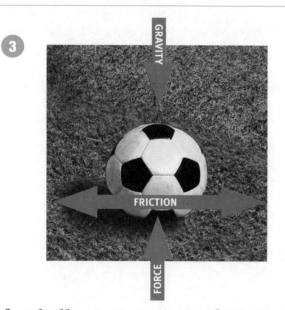

If a ball is resting on the ground, then the forces acting upon it are balanced. If someone kicks the ball, then it will move.

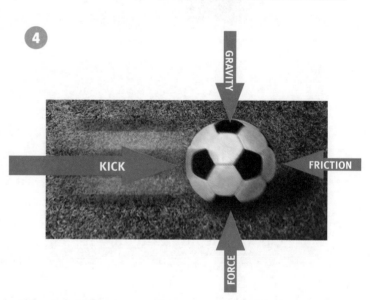

The kick is a force pushing on the ball. The ball will move in the direction of the kick.... If the ball is kicked up into the air, then gravity will pull the ball back down to the ground....

Objects may move in more predictable ways. Ocean tides move in a pattern.

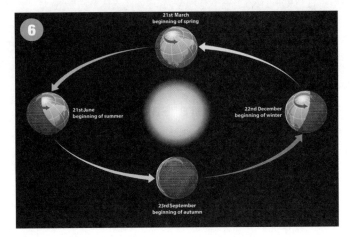

Earth moves in a pattern, too. If we can observe patterns in an object's movement, then we can predict how it will move.

Think of a playground swing. It hangs from two chains on a swing set. When the swing is pulled back and released, it will move freely back and forth....

The swing is just like the pendulum of a clock. The clock pendulum will also swing back and forth. . . . People use these patterns to predict movement and track time.

3. ThinkSpeakListen
What slows a swing down or speeds it up?

The Tortoise and the Hare by Aesop

One day, Hare saw Tortoise creeping along the woodpath. Hare called out: "You are such a slow-poke. I am so much faster than you!"

Tortoise stiffened. "Well, let's have a race. We will see who is faster."…

The race began at daybreak. Bird sounded the horn…. Hare was so far ahead that she stopped at a tree…. Soon she fell asleep.

Meanwhile, Tortoise plodded on… When finally Hare awoke, she sped for the finish line, but Tortoise had already crossed the line. All the animals cheered. Hare had bragged too soon.

4. ThinkSpeakListen

Describe what caused Hare to lose. What caused Tortoise to win?

Understand the Language of <u>Cause</u> and <u>Effect</u>

Cause	Effect
Forces cause	movement.
If someone kicks the ball,	then it will move.
When the swing is pulled back and released,	it will move freely back and forth.
If we can observe patterns in an object's movement,	then we can predict how it will move.

5. ThinkSpeakListen

Using the language of cause and effect, describe what happens to a ball when it is kicked.

The Great Tug-of-War

an African folktale retold by Beverley Naidoo

Long long ago, Mmutla the hare lived in a cave halfway up Kololo Hill.... One morning Mmutla woke up... Mmutla set off... towards the water hole...

He was leaping to the bottom of Kololo Hill when *CRREAKK! CRRACKK! CRASSHH!* A morula tree plunged towards him.

Tlou the elephant loomed over him.... "Good Morning, Tlou," he began.... "WHAT DO YOU WANT, PIPSQUEAK? NO ONE INTERRUPTS MY BREAKFAST!"

"No need to be rude, Tlou! Just because you're biggest, you think you're the strongest! If we had a tug-of-war, I could beat you any day!"...

6. ThinkSpeakListen

What caused the tree to almost fall on Mmutla the hare?

"You? You pipsqueak?"...

"Tomorrow morning, when Sun peeps over the mountain, I'll come with a rope. Then you'll see!" Mmutla boasted....

He scampered away towards the water hole.

There he found Kubu the hippo... "Good morning, Kubu," he began....

Kubu opened her mouth... she boomed, "WHAT DO YOU WANT, PIPSQUEAK? NO ONE INTERRUPTS MY MORNING NAP!"

"No need to be rude, Kubu! Just because you're biggest, you think you're the strongest! If we had a tug-of-war, I could beat you any day!"

"You? You, pipsqueak? *P-W-W-WAA-W-HHH!*"...

"Tomorrow morning, when Sun peeps over the mountain, I'll come with a rope. Then you'll see!" Mmutla boasted....

The next morning…Tlou the elephant was there at the bottom of the hill!… "Good morning Tlou, I've brought the rope!… When I'm ready to pull, you'll hear me whistle."…

Then…Mmutla hopped towards the thick bushes… But Mmutla did not stop at the bushes…. He bounded on down to the water hole….

"Good morning, Kubu! I've brought the rope…. When I'm ready to pull, you'll hear me whistle."… As soon as he had hidden himself well, Mmutla took a deep, deep breath and whistled…

Tlou and Kubu began to pull…. First it was Tlou humping and thumping. Next, it was Kubu shaking and quaking…. Finally, at the very same moment, each of them let go of the rope!

7. ThinkSpeakListen

Based on the events of this story, what do you think would happen if Tlou let go of the rope and Kubu kept pulling?

Understand the Language of Sequence

1. One morning Mmutla woke up....

2. Mmutla set off...towards the water hole.

3. He was leaping to the bottom of Kololo Hill when *CRREAKK! CRRACKK! CRASSHH!* A morula tree plunged towards him.

1. "Tomorrow morning, when Sun peeps over the mountain, I'll come with a rope."

2. "Then you'll see!"

1. The next morning...Tlou the elephant was there at the bottom of the hill!

2. Tlou and Kubu began to pull.... First it was Tlou humping and thumping.

3. Next, it was Kubu shaking and quaking.

4. Finally, at the very same moment, each of them let go of the rope!

8. ThinkSpeakListen
Use the language of sequence to summarize how Mmutla tricked Tlou and Kubu.

The Merchant's Donkey

One day a merchant was leading his donkey… The donkey carried a heavy load of salt. When the pair came to a river, the donkey slipped and fell. The sacks of salt tipped and melted away into the river.

The donkey was delighted to find how much lighter his burden had become…. He could move more quickly, now that he had so little to carry….

The next day the pair returned to the port for another load of salt. On the way home, the donkey…pretended to fall. The sacks tipped again into the water. The angry merchant…realized what the donkey was up to.

So…he loaded him up with two baskets of sponges…. At the river the donkey pretended to fall again.

But this time…the donkey dragged himself homeward with a load ten times heavier than before. The merchant's slyness had taught that donkey a lesson.

9. ThinkSpeakListen

What do you think is the main lesson of "The Merchant's Donkey"?

Research and Writing

Meteorology, geology, and engineering are all fields that involve studying forces and interactions. In your opinion, which of these careers is most interesting? Conduct research to learn about these fields, and write an essay stating and supporting your opinion using the information you have learned.

Topic for research/writing

Research focus

Type of writing

Understand How to Generate Good Interview Questions

Question Word	Example
Who	"**Who** inspired you to want to become a meteorologist?"
What	"**What** subjects did you have to study in school to prepare for a career as a geologist?"
Where	"**Where** do most engineers work?"
When	"**When** did you realize that you wanted to pursue a career in chemistry?"
Why	"**Why** did you want to pursue a career in geology?"
How	"**How** does a person become a meteorologist?"

Investigate Magnetism by Drake Conyers

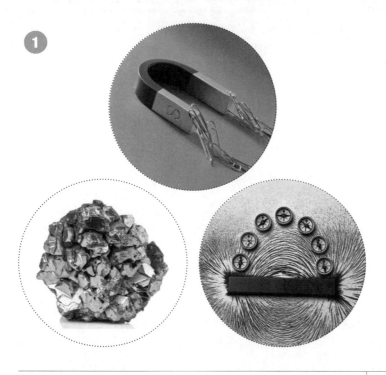

A magnet is an object that has a pulling force that attracts other magnetic materials.

Some magnets are naturally occurring. Lodestone is a type of magnetized rock made of magnetite. It can attract iron or steel....

People can also make magnets out of certain metals, such as iron, steel, nickel, and cobalt.

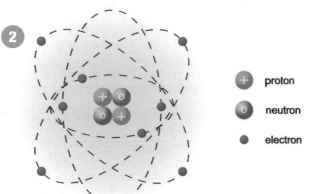

+ proton

o neutron

• electron

Metals, like all matter, are made of...tiny particles...called atoms. Inside each atom are even smaller particles. Electrons spin and float around the nucleus inside the atom.

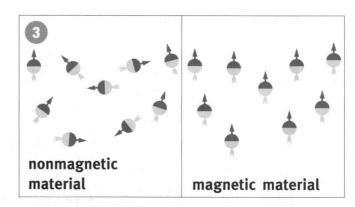

nonmagnetic material

magnetic material

In cases where there are unpaired electrons, the electrons group together. These groups can move together in one direction. This is what causes the magnetic properties in certain metals....

10. ThinkSpeakListen

Think of something you use in school every day, and describe some of the physical changes you can make to it.

4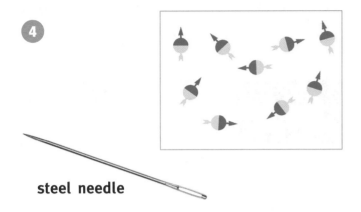

steel needle

Iron and steel are two such metals.... First, get a piece of steel. Next, rub the piece of steel in one direction repeatedly with a magnet.

5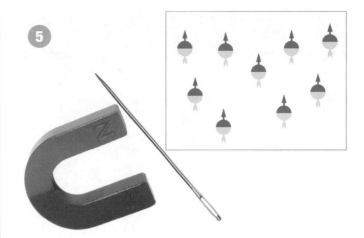

This will affect the electron particles inside the metal and magnetize the steel atoms. Finally, test and observe the steel's new properties.

6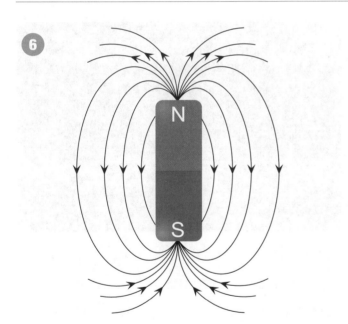

All magnets have what is called a magnetic field.... Magnetic fields vary in strength.

7

For example, a weak magnet may slide down the front of the refrigerator... Meanwhile, an industrial-sized magnet can lift a refrigerator!...

Typically, magnets have a north pole and a south pole. The power of a magnet is strongest near its poles....

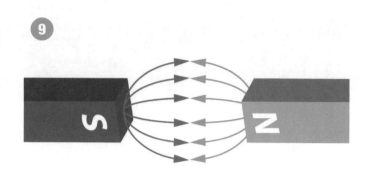

Magnets are...attracted to the opposing poles. The north pole is...attracted to the south pole. The south pole is...attracted to the north pole.

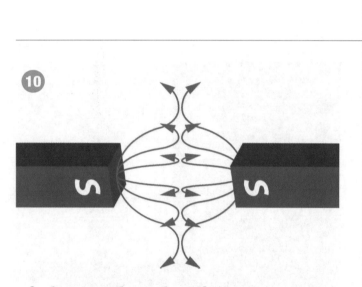

If the north pole of one magnet is placed next to the north pole of another magnet, the two poles will push away from each other. The same thing will happen if two south poles are placed next to each other. In other words, unlike poles attract and like poles repel.

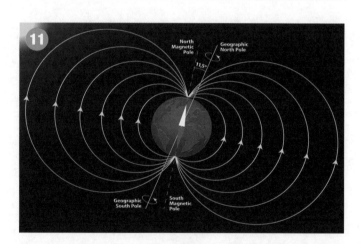

Earth has north and south poles, too. That is because Earth is actually a giant magnet. Earth's core is a churning ball of iron that produces Earth's magnetic field.

11. ThinkSpeakListen
Why is Earth a magnet?

Distinguish Sequential Text from Procedural Text

Sequential Text

Tlou and Kubu began to pull. . . . First it was Tlou humping and thumping.
Next, it was Kubu shaking and quaking.
Finally, at the very same moment, each of them let go of the rope!

Procedural Text

First, get a piece of steel.
Next, rub the piece of steel in one direction repeatedly with a magnet. This will affect the electron particles inside the metal....
Finally, test and observe the steel's new properties.

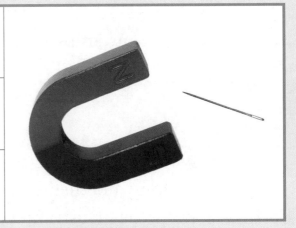

12. ThinkSpeakListen

What are some examples of procedural texts you encounter in your everyday life?

Why Didn't I Think of That?

Think of an everyday problem. It's likely that an inventor has come up with a clever invention to solve it....

You pop a frozen pizza into the oven.... out it comes. As you roll the cutter over the pizza, the toppings fall off.... Here's a solution: a pizza scissors spatula. It lets you snip, snip, snip, and serve....

Maybe you want spaghetti. But twirling the long noodles onto your fork is a perpetual frustration. A self-twirling spaghetti fork transforms your pasta nightmares into yummy dreams....

These inventions already exist. Maybe you can invent the next big thing.

13. ThinkSpeakListen

Describe an everyday problem that you would like to solve, and come up with an invention to solve it.

Research and Writing

Meteorology, geology, and engineering are all fields that involve studying forces and interactions. In your opinion, which of these careers is most interesting? Conduct research to learn about these fields, and write an essay stating and supporting your opinion, using the information you have learned.

Topic for research/writing

Research focus

Type of writing

Sample Essay

Of all the scientific fields of study that are available, I think geology would make the most interesting career. Geologists study Earth, the forces and processes that act upon it, and the materials that come from it. It is important work that helps a lot of people, and it is often done in really interesting places.

One thing that geologists do is learn about areas that have been affected by natural events such as earthquakes and volcanic eruptions. They also find out what areas are likely to be affected again. It is almost like predicting the future. According to Christopher Moroch, professor of geology at Blume University, the information geologists get helps them figure out things like where it is safe to build big structures, and how to prevent damage from a disaster like a flood. This is very useful information that helps a lot of people.

Another reason I like the idea of being a geologist is that this type of work often involves traveling to different places and doing fieldwork outdoors. For example, geologists sometimes study rocks and learn how forces change, move, and shape Earth's surface. They also go to new places and discover new sources of natural resources. I would really enjoy doing this because I love exploring the outdoors.

In conclusion, I think geology is the most exciting scientific field. Geologists learn things that help a lot of people, and they get to work all over the world and spend a lot of time outside. This is the career that I would choose.

Your introduction should introduce the topic, state your opinion, and give the reader a brief idea of what you will write about.

Your body paragraphs should provide reasons that support your opinion.

Your conclusion should restate your opinion and provide a closing statement.

Common Core State Standards

CA CCSS Reading Standards for Literature

RL.3.1	Ask and answer questions to demonstrate understanding of a text, referring explicitly to the text as the basis for the answers.
RL.3.2	Recount stories, including fables, folktales, and myths from diverse cultures; determine the central message, lesson, or moral and explain how it is conveyed through key details in the text.
RL.3.3	Describe characters in a story (e.g., their traits, motivations, or feelings) and explain how their actions contribute to the sequence of events.
RL.3.4	Determine the meaning of words and phrases as they are used in a text, distinguishing literal from nonliteral language. **(See grade 3 Language standards 4–6 for additional expectations.) CA**
RL.3.5	Refer to parts of stories, dramas, and poems when writing or speaking about a text, using terms such as chapter, scene, and stanza; describe how each successive part builds on earlier sections.
RL.3.6	Distinguish their own point of view from that of the narrator or those of the characters.
RL.3.7	Explain how specific aspects of a text's illustrations contribute to what is conveyed by the words in a story (e.g., create mood, emphasize aspects of a character or setting).
RL.3.9	Compare and contrast the themes, settings, and plots of stories written by the same author about the same or similar characters (e.g., in books from a series).
RL.3.10	By the end of the year, read and comprehend literature, including stories, dramas, and poetry, at the high end of the grades 2–3 text complexity band independently and proficiently.

CA CCSS Reading Standards for Informational Text

RI.3.1	Ask and answer questions to demonstrate understanding of a text, referring explicitly to the text as the basis for the answers.
RI.3.2	Determine the main idea of a text; recount the key details and explain how they support the main idea.
RI.3.3	Describe the relationship between a series of historical events, scientific ideas or concepts, or steps in technical procedures in a text, using language that pertains to time, sequence, and cause/effect.
RI.3.4	Determine the meaning of general academic and domain-specific words and phrases in a text relevant to a *grade 3 topic or subject area.* **(See grade 3 Language standards 4–6 for additional expectations.) CA**
RI.3.5	Use text features and search tools (e.g., key words, sidebars, hyperlinks) to locate information relevant to a given topic efficiently.
RI.3.6	Distinguish their own point of view from that of the author of a text.
RI.3.7	Use information gained from illustrations (e.g., maps, photographs) and the words in a text to demonstrate understanding of the text (e.g., where, when, why, and how key events occur).
RI.3.8	Describe the logical connection between particular sentences and paragraphs in a text (e.g., comparison, cause/effect, first/second/third in a sequence).
RI.3.9	Compare and contrast the most important points and key details presented in two texts on the same topic.
RI.3.10	By the end of the year, read and comprehend informational texts, including history/social studies, science, and technical texts, at the high end of the grades 2–3 text complexity band independently and proficiently.

CA CCSS Reading Standards for Foundational Skills

RF.3.3	Know and apply grade-level phonics and word analysis skills in decoding words **both in isolation and in text. CA** a. Identify and know the meaning of the most common prefixes and derivational suffixes. b. Decode words with common Latin suffixes. c. Decode multisyllable words. d. Read grade-appropriate irregularly spelled words.
RF.3.4	Read with sufficient accuracy and fluency to support comprehension. a. Read on-level text with purpose and understanding. b. Read on-level prose and poetry orally with accuracy, appropriate rate, and expression on successive readings. c. Use context to confirm or self-correct word recognition and understanding, rereading as necessary.

CA CCSS Writing Standards

W.3.1	Write opinion pieces on topics or texts, supporting a point of view with reasons. a. Introduce the topic or text they are writing about, state an opinion, and create an organizational structure that lists reasons. b. Provide reasons that support the opinion. c. Use linking words and phrases (e.g., *because, therefore, since, for example*) to connect opinion and reasons. d. Provide a concluding statement or section.
W.3.2	Write informative/explanatory texts to examine a topic and convey ideas and information clearly. a. Introduce a topic and group related information together; include illustrations when useful to aiding comprehension. b. Develop the topic with facts, definitions, and details. c. Use linking words and phrases (e.g., *also, another, and, more, but*) to connect ideas within categories of information. d. Provide a concluding statement or section.
W.3.3	Write narratives to develop real or imagined experiences or events using effective technique, descriptive details, and clear event sequences. a. Establish a situation and introduce a narrator and/or characters; organize an event sequence that unfolds naturally. b. Use dialogue and descriptions of actions, thoughts, and feelings to develop experiences and events or show the response of characters to situations. c. Use temporal words and phrases to signal event order. d. Provide a sense of closure.
W.3.4	With guidance and support from adults, produce writing in which the development and organization are appropriate to task and purpose. (Grade-specific expectations for writing types are defined in standards 1–3 above.)
W.3.5	With guidance and support from peers and adults, develop and strengthen writing as needed by planning, revising, and editing. (Editing for conventions should demonstrate command of Language standards 1–3 up to and including grade 3.)
W.3.6	With guidance and support from adults, use technology to produce and publish writing (using keyboarding skills) as well as to interact and collaborate with others.
W.3.7	Conduct short research projects that build knowledge about a topic.
W.3.8	Recall information from experiences or gather information from print and digital sources; take brief notes on sources and sort evidence into provided categories.
W.3.10	Write routinely over extended time frames (time for research, reflection, and revision) and shorter time frames (a single sitting or a day or two) for a range of discipline-specific tasks, purposes, and audiences.

CA CCSS Speaking and Listening Standards

SL.3.1	Engage effectively in a range of collaborative discussions (one-on-one, in groups, and teacher-led) with diverse partners on *grade 3 topics and texts*, building on others' ideas and expressing their own clearly. a. Come to discussions prepared, having read or studied required material; explicitly draw on that preparation and other information known about the topic to explore ideas under discussion. b. Follow agreed-upon rules for discussions (e.g., gaining the floor in respectful ways, listening to others with care, speaking one at a time about the topics and texts under discussion). c. Ask questions to check understanding of information presented, stay on topic, and link their comments to the remarks of others. d. Explain their own ideas and understanding in light of the discussion.
SL.3.2	Determine the main ideas and supporting details of a text read aloud or information presented in diverse media and formats, including visually, quantitatively, and orally.
SL.3.3	Ask and answer questions about information from a speaker, offering appropriate elaboration and detail.
SL.3.4	Report on a topic or text, tell a story, or recount an experience with appropriate facts and relevant, descriptive details, speaking clearly at an understandable pace. **a. Plan and deliver an informative/explanatory presentation on a topic that: organizes ideas around major points of information, follows a logical sequence, includes supporting details, uses clear and specific vocabulary, and provides a strong conclusion. CA**
SL.3.5	Create engaging audio recordings of stories or poems that demonstrate fluid reading at an understandable pace; add visual displays when appropriate to emphasize or enhance certain facts or details.
SL.3.6	Speak in complete sentences when appropriate to task and situation in order to provide requested detail or clarification. (See grade 3 Language standards 1 and 3 for specific expectations.)

CA CCSS Language Standards

L.3.1	Demonstrate command of the conventions of standard English grammar and usage when writing or speaking. a. Explain the function of nouns, pronouns, verbs, adjectives, and adverbs in general and their functions in particular sentences. b. Form and use regular and irregular plural nouns. c. Use abstract nouns (e.g., *childhood*). d. Form and use regular and irregular verbs. e. Form and use the simple (e.g., *I walked; I walk; I will walk*) verb tenses. f. Ensure subject-verb and pronoun-antecedent agreement. g. Form and use comparative and superlative adjectives and adverbs, and choose between them depending on what is to be modified. h. Use coordinating and subordinating conjunctions. i. Produce simple, compound, and complex sentences. **j. Write legibly in cursive or joined italics, allowing margins and correct spacing between letters in a word and words in a sentence. CA** **k. Use reciprocal pronouns correctly. CA**
L.3.2	Demonstrate command of the conventions of standard English capitalization, punctuation, and spelling when writing. a. Capitalize appropriate words in titles. b. Use commas in addresses. c. Use commas and quotation marks in dialogue. d. Form and use possessives. e. Use conventional spelling for high-frequency and other studied words and for adding suffixes to base words (e.g., *sitting, smiled, cries, happiness*). f. Use spelling patterns and generalizations (e.g., word families, position-based spellings, syllable patterns, ending rules, meaningful word parts) in writing words. g. Consult reference materials, including beginning dictionaries, as needed to check and correct spellings.
L.3.3	Use knowledge of language and its conventions when writing, speaking, reading, or listening. a. Choose words and phrases for effect. b. Recognize and observe differences between the conventions of spoken and written standard English.
L.3.4	Determine or clarify the meaning of unknown and multiple-meaning word and phrases based on *grade 3 reading and content*, choosing flexibly from a range of strategies. a. Use sentence-level context as a clue to the meaning of a word or phrase. b. Determine the meaning of the new word formed when a known affix is added to a known word (e.g., *agreeable/disagreeable, comfortable/uncomfortable, care/careless, heat/preheat*). c. Use a known root word as a clue to the meaning of an unknown word with the same root (e.g., *company, companion*). d. Use glossaries or beginning dictionaries, both print and digital, to determine or clarify the precise meaning of key words and phrases **in all content areas. CA**
L.3.5	Demonstrate understanding of word relationships and nuances in word meanings. a. Distinguish the literal and non-literal meanings of words and phrases in context (e.g., *take steps*). b. Identify real-life connections between words and their use (e.g., describe people who are *friendly* or *helpful*). c. Distinguish shades of meaning among related words that describe states of mind or degrees of certainty (e.g., *knew, believed, suspected, heard, wondered*).
L.3.6	Acquire and use accurately grade-appropriate conversational, general academic, and domain-specific words and phrases, including those that signal spatial and temporal relationships (e.g., *After dinner that night we went looking for them*).

California English Language Development Standards

CA ELD Part I: Interacting in Meaningful Ways

ELD.PI.3.1	Exchanging information and ideas with others through oral collaborative discussions on a range of social and academic topics
ELD.PI.3.2	Interacting with others in written English in various communicative forms (print, communicative technology, and multimedia)
ELD.PI.3.3	Offering and supporting opinions and negotiating with others in communicative exchanges
ELD.PI.3.4	Adapting language choices to various contexts (based on task, purpose, audience, and text type)
ELD.PI.3.5	Listening actively to spoken English in a range of social and academic contexts
ELD.PI.3.6	Reading closely literary and informational texts and viewing multimedia to determine how meaning is conveyed explicitly and implicitly through language
ELD.PI.3.7	Evaluating how well writers and speakers use language to support ideas and opinions with details or reasons depending on modality, text type, purpose, audience, topic, and content area
ELD.PI.3.8	Analyzing how writers and speakers use vocabulary and other language resources for specific purposes (to explain, persuade, entertain, etc.) depending on modality, text type, purpose, audience, topic, and content area
ELD.PI.3.9	Expressing information and ideas in formal oral presentations on academic topics
ELD.PI.3.10	Writing literary and informational texts to present, describe, and explain ideas and information, using appropriate technology
ELD.PI.3.11	Supporting own opinions and evaluating others' opinions in speaking and writing
ELD.PI.3.12	Selecting and applying varied and precise vocabulary and language structures to effectively convey ideas

CA ELD Part II: Learning About How English Works

ELD.PII.3.1	Understanding text structure
ELD.PII.3.2	Understanding cohesion
ELD.PII.3.3	Using verbs and verb phrases
ELD.PII.3.4	Using nouns and noun phrases
ELD.PII.3.5	Modifying to add details
ELD.PII.3.6	Connecting ideas
ELD.PII.3.7	Condensing ideas

CA ELD Part III: Using Foundational Literacy Skills

ELD.PIII.3.1	See Appendix A [in *Foundational Literacy Skills for English Learners*] for information on teaching reading foundational skills to English learners of various profiles based on age, native language, native language writing system, schooling experience, and literacy experience and proficiency. Some considerations are: • Native language and literacy (e.g., phoneme awareness or print concept skills in native language) should be assessed for potential transference to English language and literacy. • Similarities between native language and English should be highlighted (e.g., phonemes or letters that are the same in both languages). • Differences between native language and English should be highlighted (e.g., some phonemes in English may not exist in the student's native language; native language syntax may be different from English syntax).

Benchmark ADVANCE

Texts *for* English Language Development

Credits
Editor: Marty O'Kane
Contributing Editor: Gregory Blume
Creative Director: Laurie Berger
Art Director: Chris Moroch
Production: Kosta Triantafillis
Director of Photography: Doug Schneider
Photo Assistant: Jackie Friedman

Photo credits: Cover J: © Jim West/Alamy Page 3A, 18A: © Bettmann/CORBIS; Page 4A: NOAA; Page 4D: © DOD Photo / Alamy; Page 5, 10C, 13: ASSOCIATED PRESS; Page 6A, 8A: © David R. Frazier Photolibrary, Inc. / Alamy; Page 6B, 11C, 12A, 16D: Everett Collection/ Newscom; Page 7A, 7B, 8B, 12C, 14B, 16A, 16B, 18B: Granger, NYC; Page 7D, 12B, 17C, 17F: Library of Congress; Page 10B: akg-images/Newscom; Page 10D: REX USA/Underwood Archives / UIG/Rex; Page 11A: PATRICK D. WITTY/KRT/Newscom; Page 11B: Don Cravens / Contributor / Getty Images; Page 11D: Chris Travis,Christopher Travis News Syndication/ Newscom; Page 17D, 21D: Picture History/Newscom; Page 18C: Seattle Post-Intelligencer Collection, Museum of History & Industry, Seattle; All Rights Reserved; Page 19B: Dr. Hector P. Garcia Papers, Special Collections & Archives, Texas A&M University-Corpus Christi, Bell Library; Page 25B: Biosphoto / Biosphoto; Page 25D: Tim Zurowski / All Canada Photos; Page 29C: Greg Johnston/Getty Images; Page 44c,46d: Alan and Sandy Carey; Page 48d: Masa Ushioda / age footstock; Page 56d: Andy Murch/Visuals Unlimited, Inc.; Page 62, 70a, 70b, 70d, 75c: Jack sells a cow for some beans, English School, (19th century) / Private Collection / © Look and Learn / Bridgeman Images; Page 63b: Granger, NYC; Page 70c, 75c: The bean stalk grows out of sight in a night, English School, (19th century) / Private Collection / © Look and Learn / Bridgeman Images; Page 71a, 75a; Jack climbs the bean stalk, English School, (19th century) / Private Collection / © Look and Learn / Bridgeman Images; Page 71b, 71d: Jack and the castle, English School, (19th century) / Private Collection / © Look and Learn / Bridgeman Images; Page 71c, 72d, 74b, 79: Jack takes the talking harp, English School, (19th century) / Private Collection / © Look and Learn / Bridgeman Images; Page 72a, 74a: The hen that lays golden eggs, English School, (19th century) / Private Collection / © Look and Learn / Bridgeman Images; Page 72b, 72d, 74c: Jack takes the giant's money bags, English School, (19th century) / Private Collection / © Look and Learn / Bridgeman Images; Page 72c: The giant breaks his neck, English School, (19th century) / Private Collection / © Look and Learn / Bridgeman Images;Page 82: Underwood Archives; Page 83a: Provider: © Tom Grill/Corbis; Page 83b: © Xinhua / Alamy; Page 84a: Granger, NYC; Page 86b: © Bettmann/CORBIS; Page 86c: © Ted Soqui/Corbis; Page 86d: Everett Collection; Page 88b: © CORBIS; Page 91a: Granger, NYC; Page 91b: Omikron Omikron; Page 91c: © Schenectady Museum; Hall of Electrical History Foundation/CORBIS; Page 91d: © Pictorial Press Ltd / Alamy; Page 92a,101c: © Bettmann/ CORBIS; Page 94b: Granger, NYC; Page 96c: Terence Mendoza/ss.com; Page 100a: © Bettmann/ CORBIS; Page 102: Granger, NYC; Page 114: © Ivy Close Images / Alamy; Page 124a: Radius / Radius; Page 128a: Joe Christensen/ts.com; Page 128c: Robby Dagan/ss.com; Page 131b, 133c: Granger, NYC; Page 132c: ASSOCIATED PRESS; Page 132d: Granger, NYC; Page 145e: Science Source; Page 155a: Detlev van Ravenswaay / Science Source; Page 159b: © B.A.E. Inc. / Alamy; Page 160b: © Friedrich Saurer / Alamy; Page 163b: © Yadid Levy/Robert Harding World Imagery/Corbis; Page 167a: Scott Olson; Page 176d,179a: Peter Walton Photography; Page 177a, 177b: © Morris, Steven/the food passionates/Corbis; Page 178a, 179b: PhotoStock-Israel / Science Source; Page 178d: © Gapper / Alamy; Page 183b: Jupiterimages; Page 197e: © Lourens Smak / Alamy; Page 198d: Richard Hutchings / Science Source

Art credits: Page 28: David Harrington; Page 34: Juanbjuan Oliver; Page 40: David Harrington; Page 60: Juanbjuan Oliver; Page 64: Doug McGredy; Page 106-107: Lisa Manuzak; Page 126-127: Ayesha Lopez; Page 136-138: Frank Mayo; Page 150-152: Alvaro Iglesias; Page 168: Helen Poole; Page 174: Jeff Ebbeler; Page 188: Marcin Piwowarski; Page 194: Alexandra Colombo

Permissions: Excerpt from *How Tia Lola Came To Visit Stay*. Copyright © 2001 by Julia Alvarez. Published by Dell Yearling and in hardcover by Alfred A. Knopf Children's Books, a division of Random House, New York. By permission of Susan Bergholz Literary Services, New York, NY and Lamy, NM. All rights reserved.

Excerpt from *Sarah Plain and Tall* copyright © 1985 by Patricia Maclachlan. Used by permission of HarperCollins Publishers

"Jewels" from *Space Songs* by Myra Cohn Livingston. © 1988 Myra Cohn Livingston. All rights reserved. Used by permission of Marian Reiner.

ISBN: 978-1-5021-6645-6 (hardcover)
ISBN: BE2776 (paperback)